The War between the State and the Family

How Government Divides and Impoverishes

The War between the State and the Family

How Government Divides and Impoverishes

PATRICIA MORGAN

The Institute of Economic Affairs

First published in Great Britain in 2007 by
The Institute of Economic Affairs
2 Lord North Street
Westminster
London SW1P 3LB
in association with Profile Books Ltd

The mission of the Institute of Economic Affairs is to improve public understanding of the fundamental institutions of a free society, by analysing and expounding the role of markets in solving economic and social problems.

A CIP catalogue record for this book is available from the British Library.

ISBN-10: 0 255 36596 9
ISBN-13: 978 0 255 36596 3

Many IEA publications are translated into languages other than English or are reprinted. Permission to translate or to reprint should be sought from the Director General at the address above.

Typeset in Stone by MacGuru Ltd
info@macguru.org.uk

Printed and bound in Great Britain by Hobbs the Printers

CONTENTS

THE AUTHOR

Patricia Morgan has published extensively on crime, the family, adoption and welfare policy over more than twenty years. Her most recent books are *Family Structure and Economic Outcomes* (2004), for the Economic Research Council, *Family Matters: Family Breakdown and Its Consequences* (a study in the New Zealand context, 2004) and *Family Policies, Family Changes* (based on Sweden, Italy and the UK, published in 2006). She is Visiting Fellow at the School of Humanities, Buckingham University.

FOREWORD

It has recently become acceptable, indeed fashionable, for politicians to talk about the family. For much of the last twenty years or so, any reference by politicians to the importance of the family would have been greeted by an outcry from the chattering classes complaining that politicians were declaring war on single mothers or undermining non-traditional family lifestyles. Yet it should be possible to have a rational economic debate about the family, as the institution of the family is amenable to rational economic analysis. Families respond to incentives and disincentives put in place by public policy-makers. It is therefore right that family policy should be a subject of discussion among politicians.

The starting point for Patricia Morgan's discussion is a presentation of the evidence that the family is an extremely effective vehicle for raising the welfare of its members. Therefore it is quite possible that the state can best support the family by doing very little. That is by providing it with the minimum of explicit support, by not taxing the family heavily and by not subsidising the provision of welfare services to those who choose alternatives to financially self-sustaining family life.

At one level, the family can be seen as a unit within which there is enormous transfer of economic resources between husband and wife, parents and children (in both directions) and, on a wider scale, within extended families. The family is the most important vehicle of welfare and is the welfare vehicle of first resort. Within the family many services are provided by family members to each other, rarely for explicit payment. Basic economic analysis suggests that the family could be seriously undermined if the state provided significant support for dependants who are not being brought up within self-sustaining family units, and if it also provided services, such as childcare, that are generally provided within families. Patricia Morgan shows that this is precisely what has happened in the last 25 years. In the Conservative years the government increased resource transfers to individuals who did not bring up their children within a stable family structure while dragging more and more poor families into the income tax net. In the Labour years the government has been providing, at subsidised rates or free of charge, many of the services – such as childcare and long-term care for the elderly – that families once provided for themselves. The biggest financial gains are obtained by those who live together but pretend to live apart: fraud appears to be endemic, and this is not surprising given the incentives of large welfare payments that are available.

It could be argued that the driving force of significantly reduced family formation is not economic but social. Social changes have perhaps led to a desire by individuals to bring up children in family circumstances different from those of a generation or two ago. The evidence, however, simply does not support this hypothesis. Internationally, tax and benefit systems are important determinants of family structure. Within the UK, those who are outside the influence of the benefit system, because of the level of their earnings, are much more likely to have and to sustain self-supporting family structures within which to raise children.

Patricia Morgan does not simply analyse the problem, she

also suggests policy solutions. The author argues that divorce laws should be reformed to ensure that those who have made commitments should be held financially responsible. What is the point, Patricia Morgan asks, of having a marriage contract if the state then passes statute law that simply allows one party to walk away from their freely entered obligations? Child support obligations should also be strictly enforced. There should also be a reform of means-tested benefits and the tax system. The current situation whereby couples bringing up children together lose entitlement to benefits without any offsetting compensation within the tax system should be ended. This may involve reform of the tax system, reform of the benefits system or both.

The author's argument is all the more compelling because it is backed up with strong evidence and is argued from an unemotional economic perspective. Individuals within families are rational agents who respond to incentives. Welfare policy in the UK, argues Patricia Morgan, has gone wrong precisely because this fact has been ignored by successive governments.

The views expressed in this Hobart Paper are, as in all IEA publications, those of the author and not those of the Institute (which has no corporate view), its managing trustees, Academic Advisory Council members or senior staff.

PHILIP BOOTH

Editorial and Programme Director,
Institute of Economic Affairs
Professor of Insurance and Risk Management,
Sir John Cass Business School, City University
January 2007

SUMMARY

- The proportion of one-person households in the UK has more than doubled in the last 45 years, with over half of those living alone now being below pension age. Over a similar time period the proportion of births to non-married parents has increased fivefold.
- According to the Millennium Cohort Study, the parents of a child are five times more likely to split up in the first three years of a child's life if they are cohabiting than if they are married. They are twelve times more likely to split up if they regard themselves as 'closely involved' than if they are married.
- There are higher levels of child poverty and worklessness among families headed by a single parent than among families where the parents are married. The higher levels of child poverty occur despite huge welfare transfers to lone-parent families.
- The current welfare system tends to underwrite lone parenthood by paying for the upkeep of the children while the parent does not work or by taking over the care of the children while the parent works – or by a combination of both. Lone-parent families depend upon benefits and tax credits for an average of 66 per cent of their income.

- The willingness of the state to take on the responsibilities of paying for the upbringing of children where parents choose not to take on those responsibilities themselves is at least partly responsible for undermining self-supporting family structures. Both the Conservative and Labour parties have been responsible for these trends in family policy.
- It is clear from the domestic and international evidence that the tax and benefits systems have helped to determine family behaviour – the tax and benefits systems do not simply respond benignly to changes in social trends. Individuals within families are rational agents and have responded predictably to the tax and benefits systems in the UK, which are particularly hostile to families by international standards.
- The tax and benefits systems are particularly harsh on single-earner-couple households that receive low incomes. Only when the joint income of a couple reaches £50,000 per annum is there no loss from such a couple declaring their relationship. There is therefore a strong incentive for households not to declare their relationships, and this encourages fraud. In 2004/05 the government paid tax credits and benefits to 200,000 more lone parents than actually live in the UK – this is despite the fact that some lone parents will have incomes that are sufficiently high not to receive benefit.
- Because individuals and families are rational agents who have adjusted their behaviour to perverse government policies, it is clear that policy changes can bring about a reduction in welfare dependency and a strengthening of the family as the primary vehicle for the provision of welfare. The family does not have to be favoured but discrimination against it must end.

- Divorce laws should be reformed to ensure that those who have made commitments should be held financially responsible. There is no point in having a marriage contract if the state then passes statute law that simply allows one party to walk away from their freely entered obligations. Also, child support obligations should be strictly enforced.
- There should be reforms of the means-tested benefits and tax systems. The current situation whereby couples bringing up children together lose entitlement to benefits without any offsetting compensation within the tax system should be ended. This may involve reform of the tax system, reform of the benefits system or both.

1 HOUSEHOLD FRAGMENTATION AND THE DECLINE OF MARRIAGE

It does not pay to have no ties.

TACITUS, *GERMANIA*

Lonely planet: getting away from them all

Human beings may well be a social species, but household trends suggest increasing fragmentation or atomisation. Such trends impose pressures upon living standards and the environment, and are closely bound up with problems of poor child development, personal disadvantage, endemic welfare dependency and the increasing inequalities that have exercised researchers, policy-makers and politicians over the last decade or so. As individuals are disconnected from family, friends, neighbours, churches, clubs, associations and community networks, social capital is destroyed, trust evaporates, despoliation and predation spread.[1] These developments are not simply fortuitous or accidental, but are being created by government policies that are altering our demographics: policies that have progressively eradicated the links that bound families and communities together. Out of indifference or even hostility to human collaboration, by ignorance or design, these are

---

1   R. D. Putnam, *Bowling Alone: The Collapse and Revival of American Community*, Simon and Schuster, New York, 2000.

subverting the formation of enduring bonds and furthering social dislocation.

If the media are to be believed, living alone is quite a swanky lifestyle for a man who 'has a three bedroom house that he rarely visits and a cleaner to do the washing and ironing. He has all the trappings of a comfortable middle class lifestyle except one: a wife and family'. Instead, 'most nights he dines out and spends weekends visiting friends, relatives or playing golf'.[2] Another perspective is provided by an account of a woman lying dead for more than two years, with her faithful television keeping the corpse company. The following day brings a further report of someone who was left dead, unmissed and unlamented, for three years.[3] The proportion of one-person households had increased from 14 per cent in 1961 to 30 per cent by 2004. It is projected to increase to 40 per cent by 2021. More than half of those living alone are below pension age whereas, in 1961, the number of those living alone over pension age was double that of younger people living alone. In 2004 the proportion of one-person households with men under 65 was more than three times the proportion in 1961.[4] The increase among men in their thirties has been particularly pronounced; once the smallest group of men living alone, they are now the largest, with a majority predicted to be living alone in ten years' time.[5]

A more familiar aspect of fragmentation is the growth of lone parenthood. While men move from their childhood home,

2   P. Johnson, 'Rise of the home alone generation', *Daily Telegraph*, 9 May 1997.
3   L. Deeley, 'Dead for two years, missed by no one', *The Times*, 14 April 2006; 'Corpse lay in house for years', *The Times*, 15 April 2006.
4   'Households and families', *Social Trends*, 34, 35 and 36, ONS, London, 2004, 2005, 2006; *Focus on Families*, ONS, London, 2005.
5   *Projections of Households in England to 2016*, HMSO, London, 1995.

or from being one of a couple, to live alone, women often move from their childhood home, from a couple or from living alone to become lone parents. With marriages falling steeply, the marriage age rising and the proportion of births out of wedlock rising from 8 per cent in 1970 to 42 per cent in 2004, the number of lone parents has tripled. While one in four women with a child born out of wedlock goes on to marry in the subsequent eight years, a half of all lone mothers (the fastest-growing subgroup) have never married. A quarter or more of children now have lone parents, who often produce their child(ren) in one or a series of cohabitations, accounting for 60 per cent of unwed childbearing. At the same time, the percentage of first births outside any 'partnership' has more than doubled in a very short space of time (from 6 per cent in the 1980s to 15 per cent in the 1990s).

One-person and one-parent households have made a significant contribution to the 32 per cent increase in the total number of households in the last 30 years. This increase in the number of households should be seen against a backdrop of total population growth of 6 per cent. In 1971, in England, there were 46 million people and 16 million households with an average size of 2.86 people. In 2003 the population was nearly 50 million, with 21 million households and an average size of 2.36.

When it comes to living arrangements, it is now usual for a trend or an increase along any dimension to be taken for a norm or an ideal. An underlying logic seems to dictate that the way things are going must be right simply because that is how they are going, and so, therefore, it must be embraced and furthered. Often incorporated into this response is the assumption that a trend not only signifies an overwhelming preference, but is already a majority or even a universal behaviour. Therefore, it needs to be pointed out how over two-thirds of people still live in couple households, as do about three-quarters of children (two-thirds of whom are with married couples). Moreover, if something is moving in a certain direction, this does not necessarily make it either right or beneficial. Indeed, as we shall see later, the trend in living alone is something strongly encouraged by government subsidy and taxation policy – it does not result from the spontaneous action and free choice of people who are facing the full economic costs and consequences of their actions.

The retreat from marriage

The retreat from marriage is clearly a major factor behind the increase in living alone. Younger age groups are remaining single more than previous cohorts, and once in a union they are more likely to dissolve it. The divorce rate increased sharply in the early 1970s and stayed high. More years are spent unmarried and there is more childbearing among the increasing numbers of unmarried people. Cohabitation is twice as likely to produce children now as it was only ten years ago. At the same time, cohabitations in which children are born are much less likely to be converted into marriage, and more likely to dissolve than either marriages or childless cohabitations. Eight per cent of married couples break up before their child is five, compared with 62 per cent of cohabiting parents,[6] with the result that three-quarters of family breakdowns affecting young children involve unmarried parents. This was recently confirmed by the Millennium Cohort study (of babies born between September 2000 and January 2002), where the

6   J. Ermisch, *Trying Again: Repartnering after Dissolution of a Union*, ISER working paper no. 2002-19.

extent of family breakdown in children's first three years was 6 per cent where there were married parents, 32 per cent where there were cohabitants and 76 per cent for 'closely involved' couples. Even high-income cohabiting parents are twice as likely to split as married ones.[7] There is a generally upward trend in the proportion of cohabiting relationships that dissolve rather than turn into marriage: the proportion dissolving increased from 30 per cent to 37 per cent to 50 per cent for women born in the 1950s, 1960s and 1970s respectively. After break-up, it takes about two years to form another relationship, which, again, is likely to be cohabitation and which, again, is subject to the high risk of dissolution. The strongest predictor of a father's absence is the parental relationship at the time of the child's birth,[8] with little difference for a child born into cohabitation or outside any live-in relationship. Even teenage mothers who have their first child within marriage are more likely to be with the same man in their mid-thirties than those who had their first child while cohabiting: 1 in 2 compared with 1 in 3.[9]

The biggest decline in babies born to married families has been in homes with around average income. In the 1970s, most children were found in the third and fourth deciles of the income

---

7   H. Benson, *The Conflation of Marriage and Cohabitation in Government Statistics*, Bristol Community Family Trust, 2006.

8   L. Clarke et al., 'Fathers and absent fathers: sociodemographic similarities in Britain and the United States', *Demography*, 35(2), 1998, pp. 217–28. In the USA, births to unmarried couples account for almost all of the increase in unmarried childbearing since the 1980s – at the same time as a rapid decline in the likelihood that the parents would marry each other. L. Bumpass and H. Lu, 'Trends in cohabitation and implications for children's family contexts in the US', *Population Studies*, 54, 2000, pp. 29–41.

9   K. E. Kiernan, *Transition to Parenthood: Young Mothers, Young Fathers – Associated Factors and Later Life Experiences*, Suntory-Toyota International Centre for Economics and Related Disciplines, London School of Economics, 1995.

distribution, with declining numbers in successively richer deciles. Lately, most children are found in the bottom two deciles. A report on the 'drivers' of 'social exclusion' for the Deputy Prime Minister's Office identified one such driver as the rapid decline in fertility for middle and upper socio-economic groups, with a growing proportion of children born to lower-class and single women.[10] Moreover, the size of lone-parent families is increasing while that of couple families continues to decline. Four or more children are now as likely to be found in lone-parent as in couple households.[11] As the age of all mothers has risen, the average age of lone mothers has fallen, with a third of the increasing number of single lone mothers aged less than 25. Unwed childbearing was once a temporary status, typically and often fairly quickly followed by marriage and marital childbearing. Now, a new boyfriend, live-in or not, often means a new child, and a larger lone-parent family when the 'partnership' breaks up, as it is very likely to do.[12]

The big surge in men living alone is in tune with this escalation in lone parenthood, the continuing high divorce rate and even higher level of cohabitation breakdown. Between 25 and 44 years old more men live alone than women, although this reverses between 55 and 64, as women are more likely to be widowed than men and children leave their lone mother's home. By 2031, the

10 J. Bradshaw et al., *The Drivers of Social Exclusion*, Office of the Deputy Prime Minister, London, 2004.

11 J. Haskey, 'One parent families – and the dependent children living in them – in Great Britain', *Population Trends*, ONS, 2002; and see S. D. Hoffman and E. M. Forster, 'Nonmarital births and single mothers: cohort trends in the dynamics of non marital childbearing', *History of the Family*, 2–3, 1997, pp. 255–75.

12 A. Marsh and S. Vegeris, *The British Lone Parent Cohort and their Children 1991 to 2001*, DWP Research report 209, 2004, and Hoffman and Forster, 'Nonmarital births and single mothers'.

proportion of men aged 45–54 years old who have never married is expected to rise to 40 per cent.

Analysing the evidence

In the next chapter, we look at the economic and social consequences of what might be termed the atomisation of households. We find that income transfers and the division of labour in households provide important economic and social functions. We then examine how policy has systematically favoured the breaking up of households and militates against their formation. The state is now willing to step in both as 'bread provider' and child carer if one parent of a child is absent. We then look in greater detail at the economic evidence regarding the relationship between family status and poverty and try to separate cause and effect. Finally we examine potential approaches to policy and conclude that the state cannot continue to subsidise those who do not meet their family responsibilities because the consequences of doing this are the undermining of the family as an important vehicle for welfare provision and personal progress.

2 THE ECONOMIC AND SOCIAL CONSEQUENCES OF ATOMISATION

In this chapter we simply examine the effects of household fragmentation in terms of poverty, inequality and welfare. Here we simply look at the evidence. We do not make judgements about policy implications until we have examined whether policy intervention is one of the causes of household fragmentation.

Atomisation in the big picture

In the twenty years between 1995 and 2016, the number of English households will grow by almost a quarter.[1] About a third or more of the increase in households will be required as a direct result of inward migration and the rest arises from the increase in 'stand alone' singles households (4.4 million extra homes between 1996 and 2016).[2] There is virtually no increase projected in the domestic indigenous population. Here, of course, our focus is on the growth in the number of households as a result of fragmentation.

---

1   Department of the Environment, *Projections of Households in England to 2016*, HMSO, 1995.

2   *England's Housing Timebomb: Affordability and supply 2006–2011*, National Housing Federation, July 2006, and Department for Communities and Local Government's household projections for England 2006; J. Brazier, *Rising Pressure: Immigration, Population Density and the Problems of Overcrowding*, Cornerstone, London, 2006.

Not so long ago, social or council housing was seen as something for young couples with children unable to afford to buy their own home. Now, nearly three-quarters of council house acceptances in England involve lone parents or single, childless men or women.

More, but smaller, households absorb more land and materials, with lower efficiency of resource use per capita.[3] There are more emissions, more fuel consumption, more cars, more roads, more pressure on water supplies, more degradation and fewer flood-water sinks. Environmental pressure groups have advocated incentives to be single and childless in order to save the planet, yet reductions in average household size more than offset the potential reduction in resource consumption, even with declining fertility.[4] The worldwide growth in households in biodiversity hot spots (defined as areas rich in endemic species and threatened by human activities) was twice the rate of aggregate population growth between 1985 and 2000. The most important factors for sustainability are population distribution and household size. These are foremost determinants of environmental pressures and relatively unaffected by population size.

Larger units are more consumption efficient than smaller units. As average household size shrinks, this changes the economics of households. Bigger households have less consumption per person from given aggregate resources.[5] Two-person households use 31 per cent less electricity and 35 per cent less gas per person than one-person households. Four-person households use 55 per cent

3   J. Liu et al., 'Effects of household dynamics on resource consumption and biodiversity', *Nature*, 12 January 2003.

4   Ibid.

5   S. Ringen, *Citizens, Families and Reform*, Clarendon Press, Oxford, 1997.

less electricity and 61 per cent less gas.[6] Multi-person households generate less waste per person than lone-person households, not least because of the higher ratio of packaging involved in producing for one.

When people live with others and pool resources or share goods and services, such as housing, heat, lighting and cars, the cost per individual of a given lifestyle is lower. Because of specialisation and collaboration, division of labour, economies of scale and risk pooling, people can also provide or produce more between themselves than would the same people on their own.[7] In multi-person households the value of general well-being is higher than the market value of goods, since home economies add value through their own production and cooperation – something that is not included in measures of national income based on traded goods and services.[8] The *London Magazine* calculated the extra lifetime costs of living alone to be £266,000, taking into account mortgage payments that could not be split, utility bills, television licences, telephone line rentals, cars, holiday supplements, etc., although this seems to assume that couples are double earners and nobody is supporting anyone else.[9]

These factors apply to all types and conditions of people world-wide. The odds of low-income entry for working-age disabled people are very much lower both for those in paid work and those

6   T. Fawcett et al., *Lower Carbon Futures*, Environmental Change Institute, University of Oxford, 2000.

7   G. S. Becker, 'A theory of marriage: part I', *Journal of Political Economy*, 81(3), 1973, pp. 813–46; 'A theory of marriage: part II', *Journal of Political Economy*, 82(2), 1974, pp. S11–S26; G. Becker, E. Landes and R. Michael, 'An economic analysis of marital instability', *Journal of Political Economy*, 85, 1977, pp. 1141–87.

8   Ringen, *Citizens, Families and Reform*.

9   M. Baker and J. Dyson, 'Why catching this bouquet will save you £266,292', *London Magazine*, October 2003.

in multi-adult, rather than single-adult, households.[10] Similarly, the likelihood of income improvement in old age, in both the UK and Germany, is positively associated with high educational status, home ownership and moving to live with someone else (aside from a spouse or 'partner').[11] While poverty greatly decreased for elderly Greeks in the last quarter of the previous century as pension provision improved, those living alone saw a 65 per cent decrease in poverty, compared with nearly 95 per cent for elderly people living with their children – suggesting that those living alone would have enjoyed higher levels of economic well-being if they had continued to live with others.[12] In the USA, recent census data reveals how household extension is associated with greater employment and access to income for lone mothers and their children, in all ethnic groups. Employment is encouraged not just by greater help being at hand, but also through close contact with other workers. Extended households were effective in reducing overall racial-ethnic income inequality.[13]

It was calculated some time ago how a family with two or more children needs two adults if basic earning and household tasks are to be covered.[14] In this way, the family functions as an

10 S. P. Jenkins and J. A. Rigg, *Disability and Disadvantage: Selection, onset and duration effects*, CASEpaper 74, ESRC Sticerd Toyota Centre, London School of Economics, 2003.

11 A. Zaidi, J. R. Frick and F. Buchel, *Income Mobility in Old Age in Britain and Germany*, CASEpaper 89, ESRC Sticerd Toyota Centre, London School of Economics, 2004.

12 E. Karagiannaki, *Changes in the Living Arrangements of Elderly People in Greece: 1974–1999*, CASEpaper 104, ESRC Sticerd Toyota Centre, London School of Economics, 2005.

13 P. N. Cohen, 'Extended households at work: living arrangements and inequality in single mothers' employment', *Sociological Forum*, 17(3), 2002, pp. 445–63.

14 C. Vickery, 'Time poor: a new look at poverty', *Journal of Human Resources*, 12, 1977, pp. 27–48.

economic unit in which earnings can be distributed to those caring for children. If you are poor, additional household members significantly increase the chances of leaving poverty, with a strong relationship between household income and the number of economically active people.[15]

In these ways marriage performs critical social tasks and produces valuable social goods that are far harder or impossible to achieve through individual action, private enterprise or alternative civic institutions, and which cannot be replicated by public programmes. Marriage is a reliable means of attaching fathers to children and provides for regular paternal involvement over the long term, and brings together under one roof the two people who have brought the children into the world and who have a mutual interest in their well-being. Marriage embodies a set of norms, responsibilities and binding obligations for its members; organises kinship, regulates sexual behaviour, channels the flow of resources and care between generations and within communities. It connects men to the larger community and encourages personal responsibility and altruism. It provides an efficient way to pool resources, combine individual talents and recruit support from a network of relatives, friends and community members, to share risks and mitigate disruptions and losses. In modern societies, it facilitates the acquisition of social capital, which is generated as a by-product of relationships, or in bonds of mutual trust, dependability, commitment, shared values and obligations.[16]

---

15   'The effects of taxes and benefits on household income, 1992', *Economic Trends*, 483, January 1994.
16   R. Rowthorn, *Marriage and Trust*, Cambridge, 1999.

Problems in life

The growth in non-marriage, marital delay and dissolution is linked to children's lack of well-being and to the manifold ills encompassed by the soft Marxist labels 'socially excluded' or 'disadvantaged' (which explain problematic or troublesome outcomes in ways that imply that people are being denied something or discriminated against).

The rise in lone-parent families and sequential partnering (with its 'multi-partnered fertility') has occurred as a multitude of large-scale, well-conducted studies have accumulated and demonstrated how children born or adopted and raised in an intact marriage are, on average, more apt to avoid criminal and psychiatric trouble, achieve more educationally, become gainfully employed and, in turn, to successfully raise the next generation, compared with those reared by single or cohabiting parents, step-parents, foster parents or in institutions. The findings are in one direction and have altered little, if at all, over time. Adverse outcomes usually have double to treble the prevalence among children not with their original and married parents: and relatively much greater prevalence in the cases of abuse and homelessness. One example from recent work in the UK shows that children with a lone parent, particularly in pre-school years, end up with lower educational attainments and poorer labour market and health outcomes as young adults than children from intact families.[17]

As people increasingly rear children across multiple households, there are circumstances that diffuse the level of parental investment in terms of the time, emotion and resources that children will receive. Not only do fathers' allegiances shift when

17   R. Ermisch and M. Francesconi, 'Family structure and children's achievements', *Journal of Population Economics*, 2001.

they leave one family and move on to have children with another 'partner', but these circumstances are fraught with conflict and insecurity, suggesting that children in such settings will be at far greater risk of adverse outcomes.[18] The evidence relating a substantially increased risk of severe mental illness, or psychosis, with having lived in a lone-parent household during childhood is mounting.[19] The same applies to having spent time in institutional care, where the vast bulk of the care population comes from lone-parent homes.[20]

Outcomes for adults living alone are not brilliant either. Married people are consistently better off in terms of longevity, mental and physical health, and suffer lower levels of violence and addiction. These outcomes are not explained by selection of certain types of person into marriage. The longest-running study of criminality, which has traced its subjects from 17 to 70, found that marriage had the greatest effect of any variable on reducing criminality.[21] Its decline may help to explain why offenders are taking far longer to withdraw from lawbreaking as they get older.

18   M. J. Carlson and F. F. Furstenberg, 'The prevalence and correlates of multipart-nered fertility among urban US parents', *Journal of Marriage and the Family*, 68, 2006, pp. 718–32.

19   S. Wicks, 'Social adversity in childhood and the risk of developing psychosis: a national cohort study', *American Journal of Psychiatry*, 162, 2005, pp. 1652–7; O. Agid et al., 'Environment and vulnerability to major psychiatric illness: a case control study of early parental loss in major depression, bipolar disorder and schizophrenia', *Molecular Psychiatry*, 4, 1999, pp. 163–72; and C. Morgan et al., 'Parental separation, loss and psychosis in different ethnic groups: a case-control study', *Psychological Medicine*, 2006, pp. 1–9.

20   P. Bebbington et al., 'Psychosis, victimisation and childhood disadvantage: evid-ence from the second British National Survey of Psychiatric Morbidity', *British Journal of Psychiatry*, 185, 2004, pp. 220–26.

21   J. H. Laub and R. Sampson, *Shared Beginnings: Divergent Lives*, Harvard University Press, Cambridge, MA, 2003.

Down, out and dependent: women and children

The emphasis on the benefits of living alone, in the media and elsewhere, also ignores the ways in which fragmentation is closely bound to endemic welfare dependency and increasing inequalities.

There was generally a growth in the proportion of children in low-income groups in the last quarter of the twentieth century, as the percentage falling below 50 per cent of mean income grew from 9 per cent in 1979 to a high of 34 per cent in 1995/96 (6 per cent to nearly 24 per cent on a half median measure). More economic insecurity for families generally meant an incidence change, while a group with a high poverty rate grew disproportionately (a compositional change),[22] with the overall rate pushed up by more poverty-prone households.[23]

Couples with children account for the majority of individuals in poverty at any one time, but an important entry event is becoming a lone parent.[24] About three-fifths of transitions into low incomes in the British Household Panel Study involve becoming a lone parent.[25] In 1968, 65 per cent of a much lower level of child poverty occurred in working-couple families; 16 per cent in non-working-couple families; 4 per cent in working lone-parent families; and 15

---

22 *Households below Average Income 1999/00*, DSS Publications, 2001.

23 Poverty was traditionally measured in terms of units below half average income, where family income was equivalised for the number of people dependent upon this – measured before and after housing costs. In recent years, the measure has become one of half of the median income or, sometimes, 60 per cent of the median income, which is a more internationally recognised measure. The two measures lead to much the same results. Sometimes figures vary somewhat for a given time owing to sample variation. I always use an after-housing-costs measure.

24 R. Berthoud and J. Gershuny, *Seven Years in the Lives of British Families*, ISER/ Policy Press, 2000.

25 Ibid.

per cent in non-working lone-parent families. By the late 1990s, these figures were 37 per cent, 20 per cent, 9 per cent and 34 per cent respectively.[26] In 1999/2000, 57 per cent of individuals in lone-parent families were below half the *average* income level (on an equivalised, after-housing-costs measure), compared with 20 per cent in couple families.[27]

Over the same period, welfare receipts vastly increased. The main recipients of income-related transfers became lone parents, and the upward trend in lone parenthood most influenced the level of benefit receipt. After 1970, the numbers claiming income support tripled, and those receiving in-work benefits had risen elevenfold by the end of the century.[28] A quarter of lone mothers had been on income support for eight or more years.[29] By the end of the century, 73 per cent of lone parents were receiving family credit (to bolster wages) or income support; 57 per cent were receiving housing benefit and 62 per cent council tax benefit. The figures for couples with children were 11 per cent, 8 per cent and 11 per cent respectively.[30]

These trends meant that spending on child-contingent support rose from £10 billion per year in 1975 to £22 billion in 2003 (in 2003 prices), with spending per child rising two and a half times. Two-thirds of this increase, largely means tested, was itself due to changes in the type of households rearing children – or the increasing proportion of households with one adult and (as often follows) none in paid work. In the 1970s, 92 per cent of British

26 P. Gregg, S. Harkness and S. Machin, *Child Poverty and its Consequences*, Joseph Rowntree Foundation, York, 1999.

27 *Households below Average Income 1999/00.*

28 Hansard, 5 November 93, cols 589–90, and 8 February 1994, cols 219–20.

29 *Families and Children Study*, Department for Work and Pensions, 2002, p. 4.

30 ONS, *Social Trends*, 30, Stationery Office, 2000.

children lived with two parents, of whom at least one worked. By 1995/96 the proportion outside such families was 29 per cent, the highest in the European Union.[31] Only two-thirds of unattached, childless adults and under half of lone parents had any employment.

The 1997 Labour government set specific targets to reduce the number of children in poor households. The targets were for reductions of 25 per cent by 2005, 50 per cent by 2010 and 100 per cent by 2020. This was to be achieved especially via high in-work benefits and childcare subsidies to entice lone parents into employment. Assumptions were that poor children *only* live with lone parents, who are *ipso facto* poor, and that facilitating women's employment would more or less solve families' economic (and social) problems. Since it was also an axiom that poor women were being prevented from working by a lack of childcare, it was further assumed that at least 70 per cent (maybe even 90 per cent) of lone parents would eagerly rush into work given the opportunity. Such beliefs are empirically unfounded and have been seemingly incapable of being shaken by evidence. For example: one contemporary study has found that only 15 per cent of the lone parents surveyed were at all interested in childcare and work.[32]

Unsurprisingly, neither the increase in lone parents' employment nor the fall in child poverty has met expectations. Around 93 per cent of couple families had at least one parent working sixteen or more hours a week by 2003, the majority being dual earners. Lone parents still account for the majority of children in workless

---

31 ONS, 'Labour Force Survey 1998', in *Labour Market Trends 1999*, Stationery Office.

32 B. Brown and G. Dench, *Valuing Informal Care*, Hera Trust, London, 2004.

households, although they are still not the majority of families.[33] The proportion of couples with dependent children where both worked increased to 68 per cent in 2004.[34] Only 5 per cent of couples with children were in entirely workless households (not even one hour of paying work a week), while 46 per cent of lone-parent households were in this position – as were 27 per cent of one-person (childless) households (accounting for 32 per cent of workless households).[35] Rising employment has occurred alongside the continued increase in people who are neither in work nor officially unemployed. In 1992, there were 2.6 economically inactive people of working age for every one unemployed person. In 2004 this figure was 5.6.[36] The reduction in the percentage of lone parents who are not working at all has itself been offset by an increase in the number of children in lone-parent families (by about 150,000 between 1998/99 and 2004/05) as the number rose above 3 million for the first time.[37] The increased likelihood that children would have a lone parent (who was not working and who, therefore, had a higher poverty risk) added another 50,000 to the number in poverty.

For all this, and with all the expenditure, poverty declined for a number of groups: for children with lone parents; families with disabled adults or with one or more disabled children; those living as local authority tenants; those in households with

---

33 From the Family Resources Survey. M. Brewer et al., *Poverty and Inequality in Britain: 2005*, Institute for Fiscal Studies, 2005.

34 A. Walling, 'Families and work', *Labour Market Trends*, ONS, July 2005.

35 A. Walling, *Workless Households: Results from the 2005 LFS*, Stationery Office, London, 2005.

36 N. Hillman, *Is Britain Working?*, Bow Group, 2005.

37 M. Brewer et al., *Poverty and Inequality in Britain 2006*, Institute of Fiscal Studies, London, 2006.

children under five; and those in big families.[38] While the proportion of children living in households with lone parents and whose
income was below 60 per cent of the *median* after housing costs
fell from 59 per cent to 48 per cent, however, the rate for children
with couples hardly changed (from 22 per cent to 20 per cent).
A greater percentage of the *total* number of children who live in
households with income less than 60 per cent of the *median* now
comprised children with two parents (a rise from 54 per cent to
57 per cent). Children in families with the very lowest incomes
are more likely to be with couples – nearly two-thirds of those in
families below 50 per cent of median income. While nearly all the
poor children in lone-parent households are now in homes where
no one works, the vast majority of poor children in two-parent
households have at least one adult in work. Indeed, the poverty
rate for children in couple households where both parents were
in full-time work or where one was in full-time work and the other
worked part time did not decline at all. Over 80 per cent of poor
children with working parents live in couple families, where a
family with a low-paid father is nearly twice as likely to be poor as
a family with a lone mother. As a result, there are twice as many
children with working couples who are poor compared with those
with non-working couples – the reverse of the situation for lone
parents.[39]

These changes in the level and distribution of child poverty
reflect the ways in which lone parents have been the focus of

---

38   J. Bradshaw, *How Has the Child Poverty Rate and Composition Changed?*, Joseph
     Rowntree Foundation, 2006.
39   P. Gregg, S. Harkness and L. Macmillan, 'A review of issues relating to the labour
     market and economy, particularly in terms of the impact of labour market initi-
     atives on children's income poverty', Working paper, Joseph Rowntree Founda-
     tion, 2006.

subsidy levels unavailable or inaccessible to couples (see below) when, for obvious reasons, it takes more income to push two adults over the poverty threshold than one. In other words: government is providing support on the basis of family structure and not family need. By 2003/04, a lone parent working part time for £165 a week with one child under eleven and in social housing had a net income after housing costs that was £60.11 higher than if they were on income support. A couple in similar circumstances was only £29.88 a week better off after moving into work. The couple needed gross earnings over £280 a week to be at least £60 a week better off than on out-of-work benefits.

Overall, the package of tax and benefit reforms introduced after 1997 made lone parents in work £36.67 a week better off on average, whereas single-earner couples with children were only £8.42 a week better off and two-earner couples were £13.56 worse off. When lone parents work sixteen hours a week or more at the minimum wage, tax credits lift most over the poverty line. Admittedly, their incomes may not rise much farther, not least because the massive injection of resources necessary to propel them into work at all is withdrawn by means testing as income increases.[40] Moreover (see below), incentives to work have been progressively eroded by more benefits for the workless.

Trying to push down child poverty while, at the same time, underwriting lone parenthood is a difficult and very expensive business. To do so, the state must take over the upkeep or the care of children – or both. Either the parent is a full-time mother and the state the 'bread provider', or the parent becomes a secondary or supplementary earner to the state as primary provider.

---

40   S. Adam, M. Brewer and A. Shephard, *Financial Work Incentives in Britain*, Institute of Fiscal Studies, 2006.

Employed lone parents tend to work around the qualifying minimum of sixteen hours per week for in-work benefits, with their wages topped up by the maximum tax credit and childcare payments. Lone parents received payments more than five times larger than couple families (a median weekly payment of nearly £140 compared with £26) by 2002 – depending upon benefits and tax credits for 66 per cent of their income.[41] Instead of lone parents becoming 'self-sufficient' with work and childcare – and even contributing to the Treasury – it is admitted that there is hardly any financial saving – rather the reverse, since almost as much is going just to top up wages as would be paid in out-of-work benefits. Unless 'market incomes make a greater contribution, the public cost of ending child poverty will be very great indeed'.[42]

The massive subsidies must, moreover, continue into the long term to keep lone parents poverty-free as, at the same time, their numbers grow. In contrast, while couples with children numerically make up more of the poor at any one time, they tend to exit poverty sooner, are better able to capitalise on any help provided, move farther up the income distribution and are likely to stay in higher income groups.[43] Work decreases poverty, but marriage may be the most important influence on poverty status in the long run; something which – like anything else in this world – may be impeded to the degree that disadvantages or handicaps are

---

41 M. Barnes et al., *Family Life in Britain: Findings from the 2003 Families and Children Study (FACS)*, Research Report no. 250, DWP, 2005.

42 Gregg et al., 'A review of issues'.

43 S. Jarvis and S. Jenkins, 'How much income mobility is there in Britain?', *Economic Journal*, 108, 1998, pp. 428–43; and see, for earlier, D. W. Wolfe, 'The economic consequences of experiencing parental marital disruption', *Children and Youth Services Review 4*, 1982, pp. 141–62, and Barnes et al., *Family Life in Britain.*

imposed at the starting line.[44] If we do not encourage circumstances where the exit rate from poverty is highest and reinforce these exits, we have more entries into poverty than we have exits.[45]

Thus we see an obvious economic phenomenon. For large numbers of cases it is not possible for lone parents to both provide economically *and* look after the children. In the case of a couple with children, these activities can be divided appropriately and undertaken by the couple. In the case of a lone-parent family, the state takes on one role or the other. In doing so, lone parenthood is made a less unattractive option.

Down, out and dependent: men

It needs to be remembered how lone parenthood is doubly connected to the workless-household phenomenon. Increasing male drop-out from the labour force shadows the rise of welfare-dependent lone parents. The situation is familiar in Sweden, a country with high rates of lone motherhood, where single men make up about a third of the welfare caseload. In the UK, around 17 per cent of working-age men (25–64) are inactive and concentrated in single-person households (compared with 5 per cent in 1971).[46] People of working age who live alone are more likely to

---

44 S. M. Burgess and C. Propper, *An Economic Model of Household Income Dynamics, with an Application to Poverty Dynamics among American Women*, CASEpaper 9, Economic and Social Research Council, 1998, and A. H. Stevens, 'Climbing out of poverty, falling back in: measuring the persistence of poverty over multiple spells', *Journal of Human Resources*, 3, 1999, pp. 557–88.

45 S. P. Jenkins, *Why are Child Poverty Rates Higher in Britain than in Germany? A longitudinal perspective*, IZA, Bonn, 2001.

46 *Social Trends*, 36, 2006.

be in high-paying jobs than the average, but they are also more likely to be unemployed or inactive – mainly inactive and out of the labour market completely.[47]

This is an important reason why the workless household rate has hardly moved since its peak in the mid-1990s, despite the rise in women's activity rates. Over 90 per cent of fathers were in work in 2005, compared with only 74 per cent of men without dependent children. Marital status is a significant predictor of male joblessness and of the length of time men spend without a job. Like lone mothers, lone men (including non-resident fathers) are much more likely to derive all their income from state benefits compared with married men, with a four- to fivefold difference in the proportions on income support. A quarter of inactive men have come to rely on disability or other health-related benefits.[48] As with lone mothers, a low level of formal education or qualifications increases the likelihood of male dependence and disengagement from economic activity.[49] These phenomena are particularly pronounced in certain parts of the UK. In Scotland, 81,500 claimants of Jobseekers Allowance were outnumbered in 2005 by 482,000 claiming other out-of-work benefits.[50] A quarter of a million people have been on

47   D. Bradley et al., 'Distribution and redistribution in post-industrial democracies', *World Politics*, 55(2), 2003, pp. 193–228; I. Kenworthy and J. Pontusson, *Rising Inequality and the Politics of Redistribution in Affluent Countries*, LIS Working Paper no. 400, Syracuse University, New York.

48   J. Bradshaw and C. Stimson, 'Non-resident fathers in Britain', in A. Werthheimer and S. McRae, *Research Results*, Economic and Social Research Council Centre for Family and Household Research, Brookes University, Oxford, 1999.

49   A. Buckingham, 'Is there an underclass in Britain?', *British Journal of Sociology*, 50(1), 1999, pp. 49–75.

50   See F. Nelson, 'Poverty of thought condemns the poor', *Scotland on Sunday*, 16 April 2006.

benefits for five years or more and are more likely to die than to work again.

Economic responsibilities for family members provide the impetus not only to seek work, keep work and work full time, but also to earn more.[51] Marriage may also mark a greater willingness to invest in human capital, and create favourable conditions for so doing.[52] As performance is crucial for outcomes,[53] this translates into higher productivity, higher wages and faster wage growth.

The employment gap by marital status is increasing, with a growing proportion of working-age non-participants having never worked, or having last worked more than five years ago, with very low prospects of ever working. This has an ethnic and a generational aspect. High workless rates, as well as poor pay, for UK black men are related to low family commitments, given that a larger proportion are unattached than in any other group.[54] In turn, living in a non-intact family during childhood increases the chances of women having early pregnancies outside marriage, and young men having lower education rates and higher inactivity.[55] Such a family background increases the odds of the children ending up in the lowest socio-economic stratum – by over 50 per cent in some samples.[56]

51   Akerlof, G. A., 'Men without children', *Economic Journal*, 108(447): 287–309.

52   E. S. Loh, 'Productivity differences and the marriage wage premium for white males', *Journal of Human Resources*, 31, 1996, pp. 566–89.

53   P. Kostiuk and D. Follmann, 'Learning curves, personal characteristics, and job performance', *Journal of Labor Economics*, 5, 1987, pp. 533–60.

54   R. Berthoud, *Young Caribbean Men and the Labour Market*, Joseph Rowntree Foundation, London, 1999.

55   J. Ermisch, M. Francesconi and D. J. Pavelin, *Childhood Parental Behaviour and Young People's Outcomes*, Institute for Social and Economic Research, University of Essex, 2002; also *Journal of the Royal Statistical Society*, 167, part 1, 2004, pp. 69–101.

56   T. J. Biblarz and A. E. Raftery, 'The effects of family disruption on social mobility', *American Sociological Review*, 58, 1993, pp. 97–109.

Single, childless people have twice the risk of poverty compared with childless couples, just as lone pensioners have a higher risk than couple pensioners,[57] and make up around a third or more of working-age adults deemed to be in poverty. When people go to live alone, they are more likely to experience a fall in income than a rise. Conversely, virtually the same proportions of those who stop living alone (43 per cent) see a rise in their fortunes. The response of government has been to bring childless adults into the welfare net,[58] and low-paid workers without children are now being subsidised via the Working Tax Credit.

What's in the bank?

The percentage of people who have no assets has risen since the 1970s,[59] along with the increase in the indebtedness of the average asset-poor household. Over 70 per cent of lone parents have no savings, together with over 40 per cent of all single-adult households.[60] This position appears to be worsening. The elderly generally have high asset holdings, but being married is a basic factor which determines the variation in wealth holdings, and drives not only the level but also the trend in asset poverty.[61] The process of

---

57 A. Aassve et al., *Employment, Family Union, and Childbearing Decisions in Great Britain*, CASEpaper 84, ESRC, London School of Economics, 2004.

58 See the report 'Single adults become "the forgotten poor"', *Independent*, 1 December 2004, and G. Palmer, J. Carr and P. Kenway, *Monitoring Poverty and Social Exclusion*, Rowntree Foundation and New Policy Institute, York, 2004.

59 W. Paxton and M. Dixon, *The State of the Nation*, Institute for Public Policy Research, 2004, p. 27.

60 ONS, *Social Trends*, 30, Stationery Office, 2000.

61 J. Wilmoth and G. Koso, 'Does marital history matter? Marital status and wealth outcomes among preretirement adults', *Journal of Marriage and the Family*, 64, 2002, pp. 254–68.

asset accumulation is far more efficient in larger households, and married people are much better than lone adults at building up wealth. The longer a marriage, the greater the assets: the longer a separation or divorce, the lower the assets. Cohabitation does not create wealth to the same extent – probably because of the lack of interdependence, lack of mutual responsibility and lack of a long-term perspective relative to married households.[62] Higher savings ratios, as a proportion of GNP, are evident for Asian countries such as Japan and Singapore, which are more marriage-friendly and family-oriented societies, compared with Anglophone countries, though there may, of course, be other explanations for the difference in savings behaviour.

The declining proportion of married households and the increase in single living may have much to do with falls in private sector savings rates and the increase in so-called 'wealth exclusion'. Even couples without work save more than similar lone parents and are less likely to get into debt.[63] With projections that the married proportion of the adult population will fall to 45 per cent by 2021, this will have an impact on income at older ages.[64] Among women aged 65 to 74, there will be almost as many divorcees (18 per cent) as widows (20 per cent) by 2021. Divorced women and unwed mothers are at the bottom of the pile for income in old age.[65] Forty per cent of divorced women aged 65 or over were claiming income support in 2003 (and 23 per cent of divorced and

---

62   D. Umberson, 'Family status and health behaviours: social control as a dimension of social integration', *Journal of Health and Social Behaviour*, 28, 1987, pp. 306–19.

63   Barnes et al., *Family Life in Britain*.

64   S. Arber and J. Ginn, 'Ageing and gender; diversity and change', *Social Trends*, 34, ONS, 2004.

65   Ibid.

separated men were too). The significance of such developments is unrecognised, or rather it is assumed that as women ought to be in, or have retired from, full-time work there is no problem: they neither provide nor receive care, and that is how it should be.[66]

To counter 'asset poverty' the state has entered the savings business, or is trying to develop asset accumulation along with income maintenance as a way to security and enhanced life chances for poorer people.[67] Children are now the beneficiaries at birth of a 'baby tax credit' introduced in 2002, and child trust funds, with double rates for poorer parents.

The family: welfare provider of first resort

Support in old age is pivotal to well-being and comes from access to non-market services as well as income via pensions.[68] Much of the direct help for the frail and dependent elderly comes from spouses, and is reflected in the way that the proportion of spousal carers providing round-the-clock attention or care for over 50 hours a week increases with age, reaching nearly a half for those aged 75 or more. In turn, nearly a half of older people receiving informal care obtain this from children.[69] In turn, far lower levels

66   J. Statham, *The Pivot Generation: Informal Care and Work after Fifty*, Joseph Rowntree Foundation, York, 2002.
67   J. Bynner and W. Paxton, *The Asset Effect*, Institute for Public Policy Research, 2001; see also Li-Chen Cheng, *Developing Family Development Accounts in Taipei: Policy innovation from income to assets*, CASEpaper 83, ESCR Sticerd Toyota Centre, London School of Economics, 2004.
68   Arber and Ginn, 'Ageing and gender'; and Jenkins and Rigg, *Disability and Disadvantage*.
69   J. Malley et al., *Long term Care Expenditure for Older People: Projections to 2022 for Gt Britain*, Report to IPPR, PSSRU Discussion Paper 2252, Personal Social Services Research Unit (PSSRU), London School of Economics, 2005.

of those living with a spouse cannot manage household tasks, like shopping, compared with those living alone.[70] This reflects the ways in which other people provide both assistance and pressure that encourages and helps the ill or handicapped to function better, for longer, and at a higher level than they would otherwise do. In contrast, older single and separated men are more likely to be socially isolated and to drink heavily.

Across cultures, customs of young people living with their parents, elderly people living near or with their children, high marriage rates and low divorce rates are all factors that foster redistribution within extended as much as conjugal families.[71] Even where extended family living is in decline or disfavoured, generational ties ensure transfers of money, goods and services between people who live close by. Kin are bound to each other by obligations, duties and rights in affiliative patterns, predicated on the belief or trust that help will be forthcoming and reciprocated. One in three over-50-year-olds surveyed in the UK looked after an elderly relative, one in six provided care for a grandchild and one in ten did both.[72] Small groups can muster more information, energy, resources and assistance than their members could on an individual basis. Their work is otherwise done by professional social workers and care institutions. One implication of current trends is that there will be ever-increasing demands on public services to fill in the gaps resulting from lower levels of spousal and generational support, as the numbers of single and childless

---

70   F. McGlone, *Disability and Dependency in Old Age*, Family Policy Studies Centre Occasional Paper 14, 1992.

71   T. Shinkawa and T. J. Pempel, 'Occupational welfare and the Japanese experience', in M. Shalev (ed.), *The Privatisation of Social Policy? Occupational Welfare and the Welfare State in the United States*, Macmillan Press, London, 1996.

72   Statham, *The Pivot Generation*.

people increase. Already, we try to incorporate many personal services and supports – previously carried out in private realms – into the welfare system, burdening it far beyond its original remit.

Important stages in parenthood occur when children become adults, and move into the world to establish themselves or need support as new parents.[73] Marriage initiates exchanges involving two groups of people, establishing a personal social security system made available through a network of kin, and changes both how spouses and their relatives behave.[74] Cohabitation is weak in connecting people to others, and family members are less willing to transfer wealth to 'boyfriends' rather than in-laws, or to their sons' illegitimate children on a par with their legitimate grandchildren. In one study, no unwed mother received financial support from the relatives of the child's father.[75] Since divorce also reduces the quality of relationships between adult children and their natural parents and weakens obligations, children of divorce and separation are less likely to see parents as sources of assistance and receive less help, financial and otherwise, than those from intact families. While parents are sensitive to their children's relative financial standing and make bigger cash transfers to those who are worse off in order to equalise their chances, this does not apply to stepchildren.

It cuts both ways. The non-resident father is not only less inclined to finance his children, but those children are disinclined

73   G. Dench and B. Brown, *Towards a New Partnership between Family and State (The Grandmother Project)*, Institute of Community Studies, 2004.

74   P. R. Amato and A. Booth, *A Generation at Risk*, Harvard University Press, Cambridge, MA, 1997.

75   L. Hao, 'Family structure, private transfers, and the economic wellbeing of families with children', *Social Forces*, 75, 1996, pp. 269–92.

to give much time or care to an ageing, ill or disabled non-resident parent.[76] Irrespective of their economic status, widowed people are far more likely to both live with and otherwise receive care from their adult children, and they make cash transfers to them that are over twice as large as those of their divorced or multi-married counterparts. As well as giving financial help of less than half of the amount given to biological children, elderly people with only stepchildren receive less than half the informal care provided to those with biological children.

The big distribution

The demographics of fragmentation not only affect the personal fortunes of the people involved and have a major impact on the public accounts and the environment, but also have considerable macroeconomic and distributional implications. As marriage is related to a more general gain and spread of wealth among households, growing household income inequality is not to be explained simply by changes in the demand for skills or educated labour or changes to norms regarding top pay. It is also a proxy for changes in family structure. From the 1980s, the UK shows one of the highest ratings among OECD nations for increasing inequality in household income distribution.[77] Simultaneous rises in both no-worker and two-worker households both widen the income distribution and cause poverty to rise with overall income. If the incomes of lone parents are skewed towards the end of the

76 L. Pezzin and B. Schone, 'Parental marital disruption and intergenerational transfers: an analysis of lone elderly parents and their children', *Demography*, 36(3), 1999, pp. 287–97.
77 United Nations Development Programme, *Human Development Report, 2000*, Oxford University Press, Oxford, 2000.

income distribution, those of childless couples are skewed towards the top, with over a third having incomes in the top quintile. On the whole, rising workforce female participation served to partly offset the narrowing of the distribution of household earnings in the 1970s and reinforced the widening in the 1980s, with a growing polarisation of work-rich and work-poor households, as the middle thinned.

This pulling apart of the income distribution is itself symptomatic of the decline and reproductive collapse of what would once have been termed the middle and respectable working classes. It has been accompanied by the rise of a welfare-dependent class, with the children of welfare mothers very likely to become welfare dependent themselves. The observation of Charles Murray that the future contains two nations, one married and affluent and the other unmarried and poor with its casual procreation and welfare dependency, is more prophetic than we might care to admit.[78]

Greater equality has been the norm in East Asia and, while this is now receding somewhat, how it has been achieved helps us to understand the processes involved. This has not required huge public transfers and high taxation. Public transfers made up 16 per cent of overall gross income in Britain, against 8 per cent in Japan, 5 per cent in Taiwan and only 1 per cent in Korea in the 1990s (with negligible amounts for working-age people in the East Asian countries).[79] A lack of vertical redistribution has meant each income group receiving much the same share of public transfers, instead of these being targeted on the poor. This is unlike the UK,

78   C. Murray and R. S. Herrnstein, *Bell Curve: Intelligence and Class Structure in American Life*, Free Press, New York, 1996.

79   D. Jacobs, *Low Inequality with Low Redistribution? An analysis of income distribution in Japan, South Korea and Taiwan compared to Britain*, CASEpaper 33, ESRC Sticerd Toyota Centre, London School of Economics, 2000.

where the bottom two quintiles receive the biggest share of transfers. Benefits and contributions tend to be actuarially related in East Asian social security systems. Perhaps more so even than in Europe and in America's past, enterprise has been supportive to families, with allowances and in-kind benefits, such as holiday and recreational provisions, cars, medical facilities, cheap housing and even discount shops at workplaces. Civil laws have required people to support their family members, limiting the scope of public assistance programmes. With low divorce and little lone parenthood, there are few workless households and few with double incomes from two core workers. The elderly have high labour force participation, although earnings as an important source of income are falling for Japan (along with children's contributions) as pension provision rises.[80]

Income inequality may be more pronounced by age and sex in East Asia than it is in Western countries, but inequalities vanish when comparisons are made on a household rather than an individual level. 'The key to a low degree of income inequality without … higher public taxes and public transfers … is to ensure that people out of work benefit from private income transfers within the family cell.'[81] This not only maintains living standards, it also compensates for discrimination and ensures that state welfare is less necessary for providing security for people unable to earn because of their youth, old age, child-rearing responsibilities, disability or other reasons.

In the UK, the penny is beginning to drop. Researchers for

---

80 Huck-ju Kwon, *Income Transfers to the Elderly in East Asia: Testing Asian Values*, CASEpaper 27, ESRC Sticerd Toyota Centre, London School of Economics, 1999.

81 Ibid., p. 34; and see D. Jacobs, *Social Welfare Systems in East Asia: A Comparative Analysis Including Private Welfare*, CASEpaper 10, ESRC Sticerd Toyota Centre, London School of Economics, 1998.

the Institute of Public Policy Research, a left-oriented think tank, now refer to '... one crucially unacknowledged factor that may have prevented the Labour Government from reducing inequality between 1996/97 and 2003/04', despite all its targeting and redistribution, or the way that changing household composition, formation and dissolution have substantially contributed to child, pensioner and overall poverty, and exacerbated inequality. Calculations are that at least a fifth of the rise in inequality between 1978/79 and 2003/04 was due to changes in household composition. If Britain had had the same pattern of household composition in 2003/04 as it did in 1979, there would be several hundred thousand fewer pensioners and tens of thousands fewer children in poverty.

The same factors underlie rising inequality elsewhere in the Anglophone world. In the USA, between 1969 and 1989, demographic change – particularly the growth in 'non-traditional families' – may explain up to 50 per cent of the rise in poverty and inequality between 1969 and 1989, and 62 per cent between 1989 and 1998.[82] Similarly, half the growth in inequality in Australia is attributed to changes in household and family composition.[83] Over 80 per cent of Australian lone mothers access the Parent Payment Single Person (income support), with 25 per cent combining it with some employment. On average, they access welfare for twelve years and, when children are sixteen, often move on to disability

82 M. Daly and R. Valetta, 'Inequality and poverty in the United States: the effects of rising male wage dispersion and changing family behaviour', Revision of FRBSF Working Paper 2000-06, Reserve Federal Bank of San Francisco, San Francisco, CA, 2004.

83 D. Johnson and R. Wilkins, 'The effects of changes in family composition and employment patterns on the distribution of income in Australia', Melbourne Institute Working Paper 19/03, 2003.

benefits, as their children, in turn, increasingly inherit welfare dependence – the same pattern that we have in the UK.[84]

These factors are also likely to account for the apparent increase in the inter-generational transmission of poverty in the UK, or the way that teenagers of the 1980s are four times as likely to be poor in adulthood if they were poor as teenagers, compared with those who were not – a doubling of the relative risk since the 1970s. Teenage poverty has also become more closely linked to the likelihood of being out of work in a person's thirties, or not having a 'partner' bringing in money. This is, in turn, related to ill health (men), lone parenthood (women) and education. Yet the risk of poor teenagers in the 1980s ending up without qualifications was not much different from that for poor teenagers in the 1970s, and the researchers insist that 'income is not the main cause'. Instead, what became really important was the higher rate of lone parenthood, so that the growing impact of family background may provide a large part of the explanation for the rising prevalence of poverty across generations. Similarly, study of the repetition of early, adolescent births to daughters of adolescent unmarried mothers indicates how father absence and poor early parenting, as well as low IQ and early sexual experience, are important in understanding this generational repetition (which is absent for married adolescent mothers).[85]

84   R. G. Gregory, E. Klug and P. S. Thapa, *Lone Mothers' Work and Welfare: An Assessment of the Impact of Taper Rate Reductions and Related Reforms*, Australian National University, Canberra, 2005.

85   I. C. Campa and J. J. Eckenrode, 'Pathways to intergenerational adolescent childbearing in a high risk sample', *Journal of Marriage and the Family*, 68, 2006, pp. 558–72.

3 THE ENEMIES OF COLLABORATION

Collaboration: a bad press

The advantages of collaboration increasingly reveal themselves, but this is news that few have wanted to hear, given an antipathetic background culture. While 'relationship breakdown' may now be tentatively listed among the 'drivers' of social exclusion in a recent report for the Deputy Prime Minister's Office, there is still no interest in family stability. Instead, we are meant to welcome and support 'alternative' or 'diverse' and 'vibrant' new family forms – with disintegrative trends presented as self-affirming or self-justifying developments that must be embraced and 'celebrated'. In reporting the growth of millions who have no close family ties, a proclamation typically has it that '… the old family standard of father, mother and children living under one roof is a social trend of the past'.[1] Aside from the admission in the report for the Deputy Prime Minister's Office, the tacit consensus of government, the main political parties, academia, children's charities and public bodies has long been that nothing be said about the manifold implications of changing family structure, unless it be to cheer it all on.[2]

---

1   R. Clancy, 'Richer and smaller households dominate British society', *The Times*, 20 September 2001.
2   J. Bradshaw et al., *The Drivers of Social Exclusion*, Office of the Deputy Prime Minister, 2004, p. 12.

Despite its economic significance, the domestic economy has not simply been disregarded, but treated with outright hatred by prominent academics and policy-makers.[3] An important analytical model has been neo-Marxist, where human relations are interpreted in terms of the distribution of power, and any care and reciprocity operating within and between generations is servitude. Insofar as there are exchanges of income or services, or allocation of tasks, power is seen as not possessed by women and children, but as keeping them subordinate: the parallel is with bosses and workers. Thus, depending upon family members for assistance subjects someone to the arbitrary will of another. In a transfer of income, the recipient may feel 'a sense of obligation towards the provider', so that they end up supplying 'unpaid domestic work or childcare'.[4] A shocking 'central feature of social policy in developed capitalist countries' is apparently 'the way it defines and constructs families as sources of informal welfare support', and has 'assumed both the normality and desirability of the nuclear family'. Women have been made to supply capitalism with workers, trading 'housework, childbirth and child rearing and physical and emotional caring as "labours of love" in return for economic support'. Welfare work has been 'expected to be undertaken within the family either by spending some of the "family wage" (on insurance policies or at the chemists) or by women "looking after" young children'.[5]

3   M. Eastman, *Submissions to the inquiry into aspects of family services*, p. S897. Quoted and discussed in *To Have and to Hold*, House of Representatives Standing Committee on Legal and Constitutional Affairs, Canberra, 1998.

4   H. Joshi, A. Dale and C. Ward, *Dependence and Independence in the Finances of Women Aged 33*, Family Policies Study Centre, London, 1995, p. 9.

5   A. Cochrane, 'Comparative approaches and social policy', in A. Cochrane and J. Clark (eds), *Comparative Welfare States: Britain in International Context*, Open University/Sage Publications, London, 1993, pp. 5 and 45.

Thus, '"caring" work ... particularly in relation to the "dependent" population of children',[6] is abnormal and enslaving. Presumably families were not 'constructed' as sources of support before or otherwise in the absence of capitalism (indeed, one wonders whether the holders of such views think that women did not have children, let alone look after them). Now that they are, 'pooled income is wrong', or 'income dependency within couples' is a chronic problem. Instead, formal childcare or collectivised child-rearing must 'play an important role in facilitating women's full-time employment. ... the route by which women achieve financial independence ...'[7]

Collaboration: enemies everywhere

More diffuse than the socialist-feminism that traduces family care and solidarity is the view that autonomy and independence are vital and central to self-realisation. This carries the implication that, should anyone have the wherewithal, then to live alone is the supreme indicator of individualism – or that is, anyway, how the message of modern individualism is disseminated. Here the individual is cast as the entirety of his self-made world, where the 'real self' comes from introspection and 'real choices' are made in a social vacuum. 'The individual increasingly feels that the locus of all evaluation lies within himself. Less and less does he look to others for standards to live by. He recognises that the only question that matters is: "Am I living in a way that is deeply

---

6   J. Clarke and M. Langan, 'The British welfare state: foundation and modernization', in 'Comparative approaches and social policy', Cochrane and Clark, *Comparative Welfare States*, pp. 25 and 65.

7   C. Ward, A. Dale and H. Joshi, 'Combining employment with child care: an escape from dependence', *Journal of Social Policy*, 25(2), 1996, p. 245.

satisfying to me, and which truly expresses me"?'[8] Each person must develop so as to be autonomous from the past, as much as from dependency or responsibility, so that they may construct the future in their own fashion – in essence, they must inhabit a solipsistic void. Then they might enjoy what Anthony Giddens describes as a 'pure relationship', or one based only on free personal choice; unregulated, unsupported and unconstrained by any external standards, laws, demands, conventions, rules and institutional frameworks.[9] As an aspect of each person's capacity to be self-reflective, self-determining and self-judging, such relationships are continued only insofar as they are felt to deliver enough satisfactions.

The Giddens vision owes the usual debt to Karl Marx, via the dreams of Wilhelm Reich and Herbert Marcuse of complete sexual liberation when capitalism expires. Rising to pre-eminence in the 1960s, this nihilistic concept of freedom was joined to a model of people as the products of forces or circumstances outside their control. Free and full fulfilment can be pursued outside or even in opposition to social relations, while the managerial state ensures spontaneous order by getting the controlling conditions right. This deterministic model of individuals waiting to have their 'needs' met by experts and bureaucrats helped to overturn the post-war welfare state as a system of mutual insurance writ large, or a national extension of local solidarity and reciprocity. This embodied a mutualist model of society where privileges were earned through contributions. Now, instead of people acting in combination to protect their welfare and enrich their lives, there

---

8   C. Rogers, *Becoming a Person*, Houghton-Mifflin, Boston, MA, 1961, p. 119.
9   A. Giddens, *Modernity and Self Identity*, Polity Press, Cambridge, 1990; *The Transformation of Intimacy*, Polity Press, Cambridge, 1992.

were benevolent agents for engineering social change, serving helpless and vulnerable people on the ground in ways compatible with progressive social justice. This is society without membership, sense of identity or responsibility – and its endorsement soon spawned a culture of competitive rights and entitlements, where everybody competes to show the greatest 'need'.

In turn, this collectivism has been challenged by a form of neoliberalism founded upon beliefs in the impartiality of markets, the person as a rational utility-maximising, self-oriented being, and so the necessity for the free markets and political structures that support these goals. Superficially, society appears as a nexus of market exchanges,[10] sustained by enforcing a set of rules, and where people have no necessary connection to others beyond sharing the same currency. Freedom resides in the exercise of choice, as the supreme value – independently of the worth of what is chosen in terms of aims or values. The focus upon separate and autonomous or self-sufficient individuals makes these appear as disconnected atoms in a mono-generational, self-serving existence. There is agnosticism, not hostility, towards interdependence and mutual support which essentially become consumer choices. These can come to be seen, however, as burdens on the world which take up space – moving on to become luxuries that should incur charges, so that the common life becomes a pretext for discrimination.

This approach may be contrasted with an earlier and more genuine liberalism which brought together the pursuit of the common good and the self-development of the members of a community. The emphasis placed on the development and

---

10   J. Gray, *The Undoing of Conservatism*, Social Market Foundation, 1994.

expression of individuality, which could only flower through social forms, is distinct from any socio-economic doctrine about the self-support and independence of units. This ethical view is also distinct from attempts to plan the whole system from the top down – since human comprehension and control can be advanced in no other way than in the context of relations and allegiances, or through man's social nature as the basis of rationality. Where people are active participants in the maintenance of standards, this increases social cohesion as it maximises freedom – not least by minimising the problems of order left to the state. Otherwise, if the institutions of civil society disintegrate because of the disappearance of values that sustain them, this undercuts the will to subordinate oneself to any rules, and threatens the entire social fabric – including the culturally moderated individualism of the economic system itself.[11] Consequently, the state must often step back in and take on roles that civil society would previously have performed

Insofar as social or welfare programmes are necessary, the neoliberal position has usually been that any support must be targeted to the needy, or the unfortunate few who cannot prosper under free market relations – although this has not been vigorously thought through. At this point, it looks as if a curious link is forged with leftist, bureaucratic redistributionism, except that the targeting of neediness is seen as a self-limiting exercise in the face of redistributist moves to forever extend the sump of deprivation or 'exclusion' that must be relieved. The big difference is in terms of the envisaged clientele for welfare, particularly its size.

From a social justice and redistributive perspective, interdependence is seen not so much as a public liability or burden

---

11   See A. Bloom, *The Closing of the American Mind*, Simon and Schuster, New York, 1988.

upon the self-sufficient, but rather as something conferring an unfair advantage. It seems to follow that lone parents (and single childless people) 'need' more support than couples, even with the same initial income. This is because couples have an extra implicit income in the second person's time and economies of scale do not apply to one-adult households. As director of the Centre for the Analysis of Social Exclusion and influence on New Labour, John Hills complained that, as couples have an advantage in terms of the economies they can make, these 'push single people and single parents further down the distribution and couples further up'. He wants a further 'shift in relativities in favour of single adults and lone parents and against couples' in the tax/benefits system.[12] Indeed, as a utility cost or phone line rental, for example, is the same however many share the light or the line, this leads to complaints about 'a tax on single people' which, presumably, might be reversed by making co-resident couples pay double, threesomes pay treble and so forth.[13]

Although often affecting to be neutral, charges for togetherness undercut the benefits of cooperation and, more importantly, may deter people from collaborating in the first place. An extra adult's keep is hardly costless, even if the cost per capita of living together is lower than that of living apart. Moreover, the time asymmetries of living and acting alone are often the reverse of marriage, for example, since returns are immediately apparent or realised quickly, whereas the benefits of mutual residence accrue over longer periods.

12 J. Hills, *Income and Wealth: The Latest Evidence*, Joseph Rowntree Foundation, York, 1998, p. 48.

13 M. Baker and J. Dyson, 'Why catching this bouquet will save you £266,292', *London Magazine*, October 2003.

Abolishing marriage

Whatever the origins and convolutions of the (complex and often incoherent) intellectual and emotional background that implicitly, if not explicitly, endorses atomisation and household fragmentation, the foremost element has been the animus against marriage and two-parent families. Anti-family activists have expressly sought to undermine any economic, social and legal *need* and support for marriage by getting any privileges granted to married couples, including tax allowances, withdrawn, and recognition extended to different types of households and relationships.[14] This has reached the Orwellian stage of editing references to marriage out of the lexicon, led by government removing the term 'marital status' from official documentation and replacing husband/wife/spouse with 'partner', which assimilates them with cohabiters and flatmates.[15] Since the control of language brings the control of thought, which brings the control of action, so there is (hopefully) the perception, acceptance and practice of a world of provisional and fluid relationships, where men move around siring and 'parenting' children as 'partners' of essentially lone mothers. This is just about the most adverse environment for child welfare one could create.[16] Nevertheless, these 'democratic relationships' of

14 C. Smart, *The Ties That Bind*, Routledge and Kegan Paul, London, 1984.

15 'It is envisaged that Government forms currently asking for details of a person's "marital status" would be altered to read "civil status". This category would then include both marriage and civil partnerships and there would be no automatic presumption of someone's sexual orientation. Other requests for personal details would be amended, wherever possible, to ensure that references specific to marriages or civil partnerships were replaced with neutral terms.' *Responses to Civil Partnerships: A framework for the legal recognition of same sex couples*, Women and Equality Unit, 2003, p. 44.

16 M. J. Carlson and F. F. Furstenberg, 'The prevalence and correlates of multipartnered fertility among urban US parents', *Journal of Marriage and the Family*, 68, 2006, pp. 718–32.

'independent choice' unbound by 'obligation and duty', where people just 'care' as the fancy takes them (and as the state meets the bill for all this 'diversity' in a 'non-judgmental' way), are eulogised in a government-endorsed Gulbenkian Foundation report, *Rethinking Families*. Condemnation is reserved for male breadwinning and policy-makers are advised *not* to consider whether 'diverse living arrangements may give rise to moral decline, social instability or lack of social cohesion'.[17]

As we have seen, from the 1970s the main clientele of means-tested transfers became lone parents. Growing child or family poverty has been construed as something almost inseparable from lone parenthood, and the welfare system – as this meant child or family-contingent support – has developed as something almost exclusively for lone parents. There have been *no proposals* for supporting two-parent families at government level since ex-Chancellor of the Exchequer Nigel Lawson suggested transferable tax allowances for married couples back in 1986. As such, support for two-parent families and married couples came to be seen as retrograde by policy-makers. This has been felt to distract from and deprive the truly poor – exemplified by the campaign against the married couples' tax allowance. Moreover, if one spouse compensates for a fall in the economic contribution of the other, the fear clearly is that couples might resort to a division of labour and women might rear their children at home. This could militate against the attainment of equal outcomes in the labour market for men and women: an unquestioned good that has been virtually inseparable from the drive to get women supporting themselves and their children independently of men. Women's

17   F. Williams, *Rethinking Families*, ESRC CAVA Research Group Calouste Gulbenkian Foundation, 2004, p. 73.

economic independence is a goal of the European Union, which, it is imagined, might be achieved were women not discriminated against in the welfare system, in employment and over wages. *The assumption is that there are no joint resources and no mutual support because people do not, and must not, share within families.* Motherhood is now invariably viewed as something women plan and deal with on their own. The references are to jobs, maternity pay and leave, and childcare, and never to a relationship with someone else who might share or sustain the costs involved. Marriage is now deemed irrelevant to reproduction.

Mother right

The construction or recasting of welfare or family policy as a lone-parent support system had its beginning in major divorce reform in the late 1960s. The flip side of the state's willingness to dissolve marriages was the collectivisation of the costs. Under the old fault-based system, costs were largely absorbed by the parties concerned. Divorce reform brought in not only consensual but unilateral divorce at the instigation of one party. While the latter was initially meant to be justified on the grounds of adultery, desertion or unreasonable behaviour, what was unreasonable became subjectively defined. As the Finer Committee on One Parent Families observed, this all meant that courts, churchmen and governments were no longer prepared to uphold moral standards. These were matters of personal feelings. The sweeping away of legal restrictions on the freedom to divorce at will also made it irrelevant that provision for lone parents needed to avoid undermining marriage. Not many men could support multiple sets of children. To expect those involved to meet the bill for the 'casualties' created by their exercise of sexual freedom was to 'impose a stricter standard of familial conduct and sexual morality upon the poor than it demands from others'. Since this was intolerably inegalitarian, dependencies 'must fall upon public funds'.[18]

The Finer Committee called for a Guaranteed Maintenance Allowance for lone parents. While means tested, it would be extinguished only when income reached the level of average male earnings. There would also be extra non-means-tested children's allowances, since it was 'rare for an individual (lone parent) family not to suffer some measure of financial deprivation, even where the head is able to undertake full-time work at a reasonable wage', and so necessary to boost 'income above and beyond the level of general family support for all families'.[19] What happened was that the long-term rate of public assistance (now income support) was made available to lone parents as another group (along with the aged and disabled) not required to register for work. The proportion depending upon this rose to over two-thirds of lone parents by 1989. From 1976, lone parents on public assistance also profited from higher earnings disregards than couples; later raised and extended to housing benefit and council tax benefit as these came into being.

As child benefit was introduced in the late 1970s to replace the two universal child-contingent measures of child tax allowance and the family allowance, an extra non-means-tested One-Parent Benefit was created. While this was supposed to be phased out as child benefit was phased in, it persisted until the late 1990s, when it was withdrawn from new claimants as enhanced means-tested

18   *Report of the Committee on One-Parent Families*, Cmnd 5629, HMSO, London, 1974, para. 4.49.
19   Ibid., pp. 295–6.

help became available. In-work benefits to subsidise the wages of low earners with children had already made their debut in the early 1970s, and their clientele was initially seen as composed mainly of large, two-parent families. By 1979, this Family Income Supplement (FIS) was adapted for lone parents, so that claimants qualified if they worked 24 hours a week, rather than 30. When Family Credit (FC) replaced FIS, the qualifying hours fell to sixteen. Like income support for the workless, FC became a long-term benefit for lone parents (who soon constituted one half of recipients, with nearly 40 per cent receiving the maximum award).

Benefit developments meant that, at any given level of earnings, a couple was left with less than a lone parent with the same number of children, despite there being an extra adult in the household to support. On this 'invisible second adult' principle, benefits subject to an asset test were exempted to the same amount whether there were one or two adults. Even with the removal of One-Parent Benefit for new cases after 1999, two adults with children still received much the same amount of benefit as one adult with children. The married couples' tax allowance, which amounted to half the value of the personal allowance, was withdrawn in the 1990s. With no disregard applied to the earnings of the second adult, a couple's combined earnings restricted their benefits, while, at the same time, they were denied any right to pool their tax allowances.

To the 'invisible second adult' principle was added an 'invisible double costs' principle for lone parents. It is still the case that lone parents on income support are allowed to earn twice the amount for couples before benefit is affected and two and a half times when on housing benefit. The logic is elusive – it is as if couples on basic benefit somehow already have an income unavailable to lone parents, when the point of being on basic benefit is that they do not and would (ostensibly) be disqualified if they did.

Social housing moved in the same direction. In the 1970s, legislation had created a statutory obligation to house the homeless which, as much as anything else, emptied the welfare state of moral content. It was no longer possible to qualify for housing through local ties or by working your way up the queue with patience and good behaviour, since a set of central and invariable rules would override your claim. Housing legislation in 1980 provided for secure, lifelong social tenancies, and obligations on local authorities under the 1985 Housing Act to provide for the homeless who fell into priority-needs categories, meaning lone parents either pregnant or with dependent children, and 'people who are vulnerable owing to old age, physical or mental ill-health or some other special reason'. Provision for the 'unintentionally' homeless meant that a notice to quit could be served on a sixteen-year-old by a parent, and this became a fully valid reason to be accepted as 'homeless'.[20] Not surprisingly, the proportion of lone mothers heading up their own household doubled between 1974 and 1989 (to 73 per cent). In the 1990s, three-quarters of lone parents were housed in the public sector compared with around a fifth of two-parent families.[21]

In turn, couples had to pay 33 per cent more council tax. This replaced the community charge or poll tax which had imposed double taxation on couples (and treble or quadruple taxation where there were one or two over-eighteens in addition to a couple). While the poll tax was supposedly an individual charge, couples were liable for each other's cost and for that of any grown-

---

20   T. Dwelly and J. Cowans, *Rethinking Social Housing*, Smith Institute, 2006.
21   H. Green et al., *Housing in England 1997–98*, Stationery Office, London, 1999.

up children. This imposed a hefty penalty on togetherness. The assumption conveyed was that multi-occupation was a burden on the community. Previously, there had been household rates, which were roughly related to property values, but not to the number of inhabitants in any particular dwelling.

Thus we have seen a systematic discrimination against couples develop in the tax and benefits system.

The state as breadwinner: the Tory years

While the trend towards a means-tested benefit system was evident in the early 1970s, particularly with the advent of family wage subsidies (Family Income Supplement), the 1980s were the critical period for its development. Conservative governments embraced 'targeting the needy' as a seemingly efficient and inexpensive alternative to the old universal and insurance-based methods of assistance. Universal benefits like child benefit were decreed 'wasteful' if they were drawn by undeserving 'rich' parents above the basic benefit threshold, and soon the same opprobrium applied to the married couples' tax allowance. Real terms cuts to both successively pushed more families on to means-tested benefits.

The period was critical for benefit dependency, or as the time when around seven out of ten lone parents came to obtain much of their livelihood from income support. Transfer payments doubled to lone-parent families, as their employment fell. In 1979–83, for every ten couple mothers with jobs, there were eight lone mothers, but the latter figure fell to four by 1992–95. The employment of lone fathers also fell steeply. Payments to cover exceptional needs and Social Fund loans went mostly to lone parents, and the same applied to the maternity grant, which became means tested as it was substantially raised in 1987.

None of this was cheap, not least because there is no finite number of needy people. The costs of income support and housing benefit for working-age people went up fivefold between 1979 and the mid-1990s, and top-ups for working-poor families were up twentyfold, in constant prices.

Historically, 'targeted' social assistance or poor relief was a safety net. Unattractive conditions were attached to its receipt so that people were deterred from claiming. By the 1980s, instead of benefits being lower than alternatives, so that people had a clear interest in leaving the state benefit system and becoming independent working family units, benefits provided a basic income for increasing sections of the population on an accepted, permanent basis. They also created new classes of recipients who received means-tested assistance while working, or for their housing costs. Employment no longer ended reliance on means-tested benefits and social security became an instrument of housing policy. All this no doubt softened the effects of major industrial change at this turbulent time: but the cost was such that 'a whole generation became used to living on the dole long term, in a secure home paid for by benefit'.[22]

The vision might have been of a majority of 'self-reliant' people receiving no help from the state, while a distinct and finite minority of 'needy' people were being well looked after. As much was exemplified by housing policy, where the 'right to buy' was combined with complete security of tenure for those who could (or would) not purchase. In practice, it meant that those who

---

22 Dwelly and Cowans, *Rethinking Social Housing*.

could demonstrate their suitability for welfare dependency had the best chance of a tenancy,[23] and that it was unacceptable for a prudent, working person to occupy social housing. The result was sink estates.

The move to 'subsidising people, not bricks' with housing benefit, or the conversion of general housing subsidisation into a means-tested benefit, played a prominent role in increasing the disincentives to work as rents were allowed to rise. By the mid-1990s, only a third of families in social housing had any employment and the housing benefit budget reached over £5 billion by 2005. By 2003/04, 62 per cent of social tenancies contained no one in work, and only 23 per cent of housing association tenants both worked and did not claim housing benefit.[24] Even lone parents working sixteen or more hours a week are far more likely to be owner-occupiers than those working less or not at all (58 per cent compared with 13 per cent by 2002). These factors are encapsulated in the way that London has the highest proportion of lone-parent households on income support in Britain (still running at two-thirds in 2002), with more than a half being local authority tenants (above the national average of around a third). They usually receive no (declared) maintenance from the babies' fathers, have no work experience, often describe themselves as 'students', and have never been married.[25] As 'inactive' claimants came to exceed the unemployed by the 1990s,[26] rising worklessness marked the shift to *more* single-adult

---

23   Ibid.
24   Ibid.
25   S. McKay, *London's One-parent Families*, School of Geographical Sciences, University of Bristol, 2005.
26   H. Glennester and J. Hills (eds), *The State of Welfare – the Economics of Social Spending*, 2nd edn, Oxford University Press, Oxford, 1998; and P. Gregg and J.

households and lone-parent families, not just a higher level of *worklessness* in one-adult households. In turn, the rise in unwed births and more lone parents was not simply the result of a shift of births (that would have been) outside of marriage and more relationship breakdown among parents. There was also an upsurge in births to low-income, unwed girls.

As in the USA,[27] strong inter-generational transmission of welfare dependency and single motherhood also became evident.[28]

In turn, welfare dependency and lone parenthood became intrinsically bound up with the increasing casualisation of relationships. In their thirties, a third of teen mothers who had their first birth in a cohabitation were still dependent upon income support, compared with 14 per cent for those who had a child in marriage, 27 per cent for those whose first child was born outside any 'partnership', and 20 per cent for all women who were teen mothers.[29] Cohabiting couples are far more likely than married couples to contain jobless men, a situation which is particularly likely to produce children and then separation.[30] Underlining previous findings, one third of cohabiting fathers aged 25 to 39 were unemployed or otherwise out of the labour market in the

Wadsworth, 'Unemployment and non-employment: unpacking economic inactivity', *Economic Report*, 12(6), 1998.

27 M. A. Martin, 'The role of family income in the intergenerational association of AFDC receipt', *Journal of Marriage and the Family*, 65, 2003, pp. 326–40.

28 J. F. Ermisch, *Employment Opportunities and Pre-marital Births in Britain*, ISER, Essex, 2000.

29 K. E. Kiernan, *Transition to Parenthood: Young Mothers, Young Fathers – Associated Factors and Later Life Experiences*, Suntory-Toyota International Centre for Economics and Related Disciplines, London School of Economics, 1995.

30 J. Ermisch, *Trying Again: Repartnering after Dissolution of a Union*, ISER Working Paper no. 2002-19.

British Household Panel Study, compared with 14 per cent of married fathers (the figures are 22 per cent and 8 per cent respectively in older age groups).[31] The picture is similar in the USA, where poverty and public assistance rates for children in cohabiting households have been close to those for lone mothers.[32]

Greater casualisation of relationships also meant less child support from non-resident fathers who also visit children infrequently.

The state as child carer: the Brown revolution

While lone mothers may have been seen as the neediest of the needy in the Thatcher years, New Labour's onslaught on child poverty in the late 1990s put them firmly in the vanguard of the gender revolution and provided the opportunity to fully realise and vindicate the stand-alone mother as the fundamental family form. The 'assumption that men are financially responsible for families' is at 'the root of women's disadvantage in the labour market', and thwarts the ability of 'women alone to provide adequately for themselves and their children', according to Anna Coote, Harriet Harman and Patricia Hewitt.[33] Chancellor Gordon

---

31 K. Kiernan and G. Mueller, *The Divorced and Who Divorces?*, CASEpaper 7, Centre for Analysis of Social Exclusion, May 1998. See also S. McRae, *Cohabiting Mothers*, Policy Studies Institute, London, 1993; K. E. Kiernan and V. Estaugh, *Cohabitation: Extra Marital Childbearing and Social Policy*, Family Policy Studies Centre, London, 1993.

32 W. D. Manning and D. T. Lichter, 'Parental cohabitation and children's economic well-being', *Journal of Marriage and the Family*, 58, 1996, pp. 998–1010, and W. Manning and S. Brown, 'Children's economic well-being in married and cohabiting parent families', *Journal of Marriage and the Family*, 65, 2006, pp. 953–62.

33 A. Coote, H. Harman and P. Hewitt, *The Family Way*, Institute of Public Policy Research, 1990, p. 36.

Brown was lauded for ending measures 'under which married couples with children can expect fiscal encouragement and is intent on making women independent financial actors'. The 'treatment of a married couple as a single financial unit ... [is] to be discouraged', along with any 'predisposition in favour of the nuclear family (which radical theory saw as damaging and inhibiting)'.[34] The remaining portion of the married couples' tax allowance was swept away. Higher in-work benefits and childcare came in to enable lone parents to rise out of poverty and improve their children's life chances.

By 2005, parents with earnings of £5,220 or less qualified for the maximum childcare credit of £10,920 a year for two children (£6,370 for one child), thus subsidising people whose earnings are less than the cost of minding their children. This credit rose to 80 per cent of childcare costs of £175 and £300 per week for one and two children respectively in 2006.[35] The lowest-earning parents with two children receive childcare costs up to £240 per week. There is also an extra £40 per week benefit paid for a year to lone parents who return to work, pushing their minimum wage to £12 per hour. The only other targets of this largesse are the 7.5 per cent of the population on incapacity benefits. Lately, lone parents on income support have been promised an extra £20 a week if they agree to be 'trained'.

There is an old Bolshevik ring to it all: women bear children by a variety of fathers, and the children are reared at public expense in nurseries while their mothers engage in some kind of state-funded activity. In terms of Child Tax Credit and the Working Tax Credit alone, the cost in 2003/04 was £13.5 billion. As the income

---

34   J. Lloyd, 'Gordon Brown, the great feminist', *New Statesman*, 30 August 1999.
35   HM Treasury, *Pre-Budget Report*, November 2004.

growth of lone parents exceeded the national average, a low-income, part-time working lone parent (without childcare costs) saw a rise in real income of 7 per cent between 1988 and 1997, 39 per cent between 1997 and 2002 and 11 per cent between 2002 and 2004. For a non-working lone parent, these figures were 4 per cent, 33 per cent and 6 per cent.

The proportion of child-contingent support going to lone parents also increased. As a proportion of disposable income this rose from an average of 14.7 per cent to 32.7 per cent for lone parents with one child, but from 3.4 per cent to just 5.7 per cent for one-child couples between 1975 and 2003.[36]

Helping a woman raise children alone is likely to cost between £71,000 and £123,000 over a ten-year period. A two-parent family still paid over twice as much in tax in real terms as they would have done in the 1960s, even with the new so-called tax credits. Single taxpayers with no dependants paid much the same. Should a couple with two children and one earner earning £480 gross per week split up, the cost to the Treasury is between £10,030 and £13,514 annually (depending on rent levels) in benefits and lost taxes. Should this be a two-earner couple (earning respectively £280 and £180 per week), then depending on rents, the loss will be between £3,612 and £8,437.[37] More children and childcare costs are likely to push the losses higher.

Work incentives have continually clashed with poverty reduction targets, since work-related benefits hardly move households

36 S. Adam and M. Brewer, *Supporting Families: The financial costs and benefits of children since 1975*, Polity Press for the Joseph Rowntree Foundation, 2004; also S. Adam, M. Brewer and H. Reed, *The Benefits of Parenting: Government financial support for families with children since 1975*, Institute for Fiscal Studies Commentary 90, 2002.

37 *CARE Research Used in Tax Credits Debate*, CARE, London, 2006.

with no work over the poverty line. Clearly, child poverty has not been cured by lone parents all rushing into work, and it was incredibly naive to believe that it ever could be. While more lone parents may be in work compared with ten years ago, calculations suggest that the target of 70 per cent (let alone 90 per cent) in employment will be impossible to reach.[38]

The government had already given large out-of-work as well as in-work benefit increases, particularly for young children, between 1998 and 2000. This has been followed by the breaking of the link between receiving tax credits and working. The 'families' part of the Working Families Tax Credit was separated off as the Child Tax Credit and paid irrespective of employment. By 2004/05, a non-working parent would receive tax credits of £3,800 per year for two children and £5,430 for three children on top of income support and other benefits.

While the government had aimed to 'make work pay', the result of bigger benefits for workless households has been to reduce the incentives to work which had been initially strengthened in the 1990s (after their weakening in the 1980s).[39] Disability benefits for children (paid on top of other benefits) have also been significantly raised, extended to cover behavioural disorders, and accompanied by an extended range of passport benefits (access to the free goods and services that come with welfare entitlements), including cheap TV licences and grants for household goods. Access to disability payments can double income for non-working lone parents, and over a third are said to have a sick or disabled

---

38 N. Hillman, *Is Britain Working?*, Bow Group, 2005.
39 S. Adam, M. Brewer and A. Shephard, *Financial Work Incentives in Britain*, Institute of Fiscal Studies, 2006.

child (5 per cent have two or more).[40] It is a depressingly familiar story, repeated in Australia – where substantial benefit increases for mothers out of as well as in work meant that any enhancement of work incentives was minimal. Instead, far more people have been brought into the expanded welfare system where it is advantageous to stay, not least because of all the burgeoning passport benefits.[41]

The CSA

Any requirement that non-resident parents pay anything towards the cost of children they do not live with has been tacitly abandoned. This process covered both the Brown and the Conservative years. Legislation in 1991 had established a formula for calculating an absent parent's liability, and moved it from the courts to an administrative Child Support Agency. The rules for the calculation of liabilities were extraordinarily complex, little in the way of penalties was imposed for non-compliance, mothers could evade naming the father by citing a perceived threat to their personal safety, the sums involved were continually whittled down, and the circumstances of appeal endlessly extended. In only about 30 per cent of cases referred to the CSA was full payment made. A simplified system later changed the formula in 1995 to reduce the burden on fathers and their new families, with even less

---

40   P. N. Cohen and M. Petrescu-Prahova, 'Gendered living arrangements among children with disabilities', *Journal of Marriage and the Family*, 68, 2006, pp. 630–38.

41   R. G. Gregory, E. Klug and P. S. Thapa, *Lone Mothers' Work and Welfare: An Assessment of the Impact of Taper Rate Reductions and Related Reforms*, Australian National University, Canberra, 2005.

collected.[42] Furthermore, a working mother could receive (non-taxable) income from an absent father, which does not reduce the amount she is able to claim from the state (unless she is on income support). Previously she could only keep a token amount if she was on any means-tested benefits.

The CSA proved to be 'one of the most controversial and unworkable pieces of legislation in living memory',[43] and little more than a blip on the curve of the progressive socialisation of the costs of child-rearing. Terrified of adverse publicity, the agency cowered before fathers' rights pressure groups (men were said to have committed suicide when faced with child support demands), any and every excuse was used to avoid chasing non-payment, and the trend towards 'multi-partnered fertility' made its task increasingly impractical.[44] But was it ever seriously meant to collect maintenance, particularly if this was to reimburse the state for benefit money, since it has been tacitly accepted that the upkeep of lone parents and their children is overwhelmingly a public responsibility?

Maintenance payments are totally disregarded for working lone parents on tax credits, with the result that separated parents are allowed a significant measure of income pooling without any loss of benefits, which they would not be allowed if married or 'living together as husband and wife'. This is hardly fair to

---

42 Non-resident parents are now required to pay 15 per cent of their net income for one child, 20 per cent for two and 25 per cent for three or more (and reducing to 12.5 per cent where there are new or stepchildren), with allowances for travel and accommodation costs involved in maintaining contact.

43 P. Daniel and J. Watts, *Children and Social Policy*, Palgrave, 1998, pp. 70–71.

44 Sir David Henshaw's Report to the Secretary of State for Work and Pensions, *Recovering Child Support: Routes to Responsibility*, Presented to Parliament by the Secretary of State for Work and Pensions, Cm. 6894, 2006.

lone parents who do not get maintenance, or to parents who live together where money passes between resident fathers and mothers. All of a resident father's earnings are offset against the eligibility of the family for benefits; at the same time there is no tax allowance for a second, non-working adult and the father is taxed as a single, childless man.

Consequences of the policies pursued since the early 1980s

There are claims that 'single mothers need to work more for the same income as coupled parents ...'[45] In reality, a lone parent needs to work considerably *fewer* hours. A couple with two children needs to work 74 hours a week at the minimum wage to clear poverty after housing costs. In contrast, a lone parent with one child working only sixteen hours at the minimum wage is already above the poverty line both on an after- and a before-housing-costs basis.[46] On an after-housing-costs basis, a lone parent with two children and in social housing working sixteen hours would have needed to earn only £78 a week in 2004/05. A comparable couple would have needed to earn £325 per week, or more than four times as much – an increase from three times as much in 2003/04. In 2004/05, a couple on the poverty line with an income of £325 per week would have received £60.77 per week in tax credits. A lone parent working sixteen hours at the minimum wage would have received £132.79 per week in

45 S. Duncan and R. Edwards, 'Afterword', in S. Duncan and R. Edwards (eds), *Single Mothers in an International Context: Mothers or Workers?*, UCL Press, London, 1997, p. 272.

46 M. Evans and J. Scarborough, *Can Current Policy End Child Poverty by 2020?*, Joseph Rowntree Foundation, York, 2006.

tax credits and have an after-housing-costs income of £200 per week, or £14 above the poverty line.[47] Child poverty among 'in-work' couple families is increasing because tax credits have taken no account of the financial needs of two adults compared with one.

In 2004/05, a couple with two children where the mother was earning £10,000 and the father £25,000 per year would be 22 per cent better off if the mother claimed as a lone parent rather than as a couple (£6,017 could be claimed in tax credits if the couple lived separately compared with £544 when their incomes are combined into one household income). If the mother had no earnings and the father earned £20,000 per year, they would be 22.6 per cent better off if they split (£6,839 in benefits and tax credits if they lived separately compared with £2,317 if they lived together). If the mother earned £5,000 and the father earned £15,000, they would be 36.4 per cent better off if they split (£7,785 in tax credits compared with £2,317). Of course, extra housing space would be needed to accommodate the couple if they lived separately, but housing benefit and council tax benefit take care of the extra costs here. Add these in and couples with a parent working full time at the minimum wage, or at average income, are still worse off when they live together than if they split up – to the tune of £260 per week.[48] Only when joint incomes reach £50,000 per year is there no loss from being a couple.

This is all without taking account of the effect of passport benefits – in particular free school meals. For example: 'in-work'

47   D. Draper and L. Beighton, *Supplementary Evidence to the Select Committee Inquiry into Child Poverty*, HC 85-III, February 2004; also D. Draper and L. Beighton, *Restructuring Tax Credits*, CARE, 2006.

48   *CARE Research Used in Tax Credits Debate*.

couple families do not receive free school meals even when they have an income well below the poverty line.

The nature of means testing also impacts disproportionately on middle-income families, rather than the 'rich', since benefits taper off as income rises. The outcome of concentrating welfare on the 'needy', while giving no special tax allowances to single earners within families, is the flattening of a large bracket of net family income as gross family income rises. Many middle-income, single-earner families have net incomes close to those of families whose much lower gross incomes are topped up through tax credits and welfare benefits. These families on low incomes, in turn, have net incomes close to those of families that rely entirely on income provision from the state.

Two-parent families may be better at pulling themselves out of poverty over time and at raising their fortunes. It is tragic that they should be so hamstrung, or heavily discriminated against, so that it is made extra hard for them to raise their status – as well as often financially inadvisable unless their income takes them out of the reach of the welfare system altogether. Since tax credits are clearly not reducing the number of children in poverty at any one time who are living in couple families, particularly working couple families, the number of children in poverty living in 'in-work' couple families is predicted to increase from 1.4 to 1.8 million by 2010.[49]

Faking it

In the circumstances, it is hardly surprising that people actually living together while pretending to live apart, in order to take

---

49   This is after housing costs. The figure is 1 million on a before-housing-costs basis. Ibid.

the best advantage of the tax and benefit structure, account for over a quarter of all (identified) income support overpayment due to fraud.[50] In 2004/05, the government paid tax credits and benefits to 200,000 more lone parents than actually lived in the UK. The government supported 2.1 million parents when evidence suggested that there were only 1.9 million in the whole population.

Discrepancies between the £15 billion that the government estimated it paid to families and the £10 billion declared by families to researchers cast doubt on poverty figures, particularly claims about lone-parent poverty, with the government being advised to 'urgently review the quality of the data used to measure poverty'.[51]

The temptation to pretend to live alone is enormous, considering the sums involved (see below), and is particularly acute when the lone parent is on out-of-work benefits or a low wage. Joint income has to reach something like £50,000 gross for there to be no loss from declaring a relationship. When a couple split up and live apart (or pretend to do so) the man's income does not count against the mother's benefit entitlement. If the man is not earning, there is still an incentive to split up, since the man can then draw benefits in his own right as a non-wage earner, and have his own subsidised housing. Alternatively, if the couple pretend to split up, the man can receive benefit in his own right and live rent-free in the council house provided for her 'fatherless' children, while, perhaps, declaring that he lives with his parents.[52] If he also has a

---

50 Department of Work and Pensions, Analytical Services Directorate, *The Results of the Area Benefit Review and the Quality Support Team from April 2000 to March 2001: Fraud and Error in Claims for Income Support and Jobseekers Allowance*, 2002.

51 M. Brewer and J. Shaw, *How Many Lone Parents Are Receiving Tax Credits*, IFS Briefing Note 70, 2006.

52 C. Midgley, 'Who's the daddy? Get lost', *The Times*, 24 July 2006.

Financial gain from 'faking it': mother and father both unemployed

- Lone mother on income support/Jobseekers Allowance in 2006/07, two children under eleven: total benefit per week after all housing costs would be £171.90 per week (approx. £8,939 per annum)
- Boyfriend on income support/Jobseekers Allowance, has council flat elsewhere: total income after own housing costs (not including possible rent income from illegally subletting his own place) £57.45 per week (approx. £2,987 per annum)
- If they lived as an undeclared couple living in the mother's accommodation their income would be a total of: £11,926 per annum
- If the lone mother and boyfriend declared their relationship and claimed income support as a couple, their total income would be £204.55 per week or £10,638 per annum: a loss of £1,288 per annum (not including possible rent from sublet)

Financial gain from 'faking it': boyfriend on low income

- If the boyfriend worked 30 hours at minimum wage, income would be £103.12 per week or £5,418 per annum after tax and benefits. The total for the couple would be £14,357 per annum
- If the couple declared their relationship their total income would be £234.56 per week or £12,197 per annum, a loss of £2,160 per annum (not including possible rent from sublet) from declaring their relationship

Financial gain from 'faking it': boyfriend on medium income

- If the boyfriend earned £380 per week (£19,760 per annum gross), he would receive a net income of £291.53 per week or £15,159 per annum. He now has no housing subsidy. He gives an address as that of his parents but lives with the lone mother in her council property. The total income for the couple would be £24,098 per annum
- If the couple declared their 'live-in' status, their income would be £290 per week or £15,080 per annum after housing costs as local authority tenants, a loss of £9,018 per annum (approximately the total level of the mother's benefit income, all of which would be lost)

Financial gain from 'faking it': boyfriend on medium income, mother on low income

- If the lone mother finds a job paying £200 per week, she nets £228.65 per week after housing costs, or £11,921 per annum
- If her relationship with the live-in boyfriend on £15,159 per annum is undeclared their total income is £27,080 per annum
- If they declared their relationship, their total income would be £448 per week or £23,296 per annum after rent or housing costs, a loss of £3,584 per annum. The loss is much less here because the mother is earning more of her net income, rather than receiving it in the form of benefits.

Source: Tax Benefit Model Tables, 2006 National Statistics

It should be noted that these cash benefits from a couple splitting up would also arise if the couple were honest about splitting up. In such a case, however, there would be additional living costs to be borne. The biggest incentive to make false claims about relationships occurs when one of the partners is working. There are therefore very strong incentives, if the father is offered employment, either to refuse the job, hide the relationship or receive wage payments in cash.

council property, this can be sublet and the rent pocketed. Geoff Dench and colleagues report how 'strategic single parenthood' was commonplace in their investigation. For example:

> We interviewed her [Francesco Dacosta] in a converted second floor flat from which she was hoping to move. There was a man present ... but she did not want him to be recorded as living there. She insisted that she had boyfriends to stay only occasionally, and lived most of the time just with her children. She had never worked, and said that she could only just make ends meet. So she felt entitled to conceal her friend's existence in order to protect her benefits and her children's well being.
>
> Melissa Terry ... did acknowledge the existence of a steady boyfriend who was in her flat ... The boyfriend was a visiting partner, said to stay occasionally but to be living elsewhere most of the time with friends. No one in Melissa's household was a wage earner. Nor was the boyfriend ... again the pattern of residence can be seen as tactically linked to safeguarding income from benefits.[53]

53   G. Dench, K. Gavron and M. Young, *The New East End*, Profile Books, London, 2006, p. 109.

In this east London study, it was axiomatically accepted as a fact of life that people maintained separate residences in order to maximise benefits. Even amicably married women and their children were declared as living separately from their husbands to ensure that they received more money. One of the researchers referred to a culture of working the housing market among lone mothers in inner London that had come to light in another investigation. Actual or prospective lone motherhood was the key (*sic*) – not only to getting housed as a vulnerable person who could not be turned away, but to property ownership under the 'right to buy' rule.[54] There appeared to be worldwide knowledge of this opportunity to acquire a property in an expensive location in the UK, which the woman would often sell on as soon as practicable and depart with a handy capital sum.

Summary

There has been a systematic and sustained attack on what might be termed 'intra-household' collaboration by successive governments. The transfers that individuals make between themselves within households could be regarded as the first line of welfare in society, yet these are penalised through changes to the tax and benefits systems. If an earning family member leaves the family setting, or does not stay with a pregnant wife or girlfriend, then, in general, the state will substitute for that earner. Increasingly, the state will act as both breadwinner for a lone parent with children and as child carer. There are few financial incentives to household formation among those on lower incomes. While the issue

---

54 Personal communication.

of incentives will be discussed below, one observation is worth making here: if it is the case that incentives within the tax and benefits system do not affect behaviour, then this does not accord with the evidence. Lone parenthood is much more common among those groups whose income levels and expectations of income levels lead them to be trapped within the benefits system than it is among those on much higher incomes. Furthermore, it is already clear that the incentives are strong enough for people to be willing to commit fraud and pretend to be lone parents when they are, in fact, part of a couple. Of course, cause and effect are difficult to separate, as is the impact of other influences. Nevertheless, it is clear that, for large parts of the population, the government penalises collaboration within households and penalises household formation itself.

4 CAUSE AND EFFECT

Coincidence?

Historically, poor economic circumstances often led people to forgo marriage and even desert families. Unwed women usually remained childless, whether they lived as servants or in cloisters. The pattern for centuries was that low-paid and casually employed men often did not marry because they could not afford to establish a family household. Non-marital and marital fertility declined together during the Great Depression of the mid-twentieth century. This is itself evidence that people do respond to economic incentives in their family decisions. This is happening today, with the behavioural response to differential welfare payments that allow a man to father children by different women with the women being able to meet the costs of children from elsewhere.[1]

Couples dependent upon one wage pay taxes that are far greater than their share of benefits and which are disproportionately high in relation to their numbers. This is mainly because transfers of income within the household exclude the recipient from the possibility of benefits. If that recipient were to leave the household then he or she would be entitled to benefits. It may be

---

1 M. S. Bernstam and P. L. Swan, 'Malthus and the evolution of the welfare state: an essay on the second invisible hand', Working Paper 89-012, Australian Graduate School of Management, University of New South Wales, 1989.

countered that benefits should be aimed at low-income house-holds and not at low-income individuals within high-income households. The problem with this argument is that it implicitly assumes that behaviour is not affected by the tax and benefits system.

Do people respond to incentives?

The Poor Law once made welfare lower than the lowest wage to encourage work and not dependence. The perceived cruelty of such a system may be one reason why the role of incentives in driving welfare dependency and family fragmentation is now denied with such vigour and venom. Does it not blame the poor for pathological behaviour, even if only indirectly because of the perverse incentives of welfare programmes? Now couples with children are 'less eligible' or receive lower levels of help compared with that going to lone parents. Because the majority of lone parents are in receipt of benefits, they are subject to marriage penalties. The advantages of living apart are set to increase substantially if parents out of work, as well as in employment, have the right to receive income from each other, untaxed, on top of full benefits, so long as they do not (ostensibly) live together. Sir David Henshaw's report to the Secretary of State for Work and Pensions on child support, which proposed that lone mothers on all benefits keep all maintenance, claims that research shows 'little evidence' that this might increase relationship breakdown. (The issue of reduced relationship formation is ignored.) Why? It seems that when respondents were asked the main reason for separating from their partner, 'no client said that it was because they would be better off financially'. Well, they would, wouldn't they? Survey 'evidence' of this type is hardly reliable.[2]

But does the tax and benefit system *actually* discourage marriage and interdependence? An association or correlation does not necessarily imply causation, even if it seems obvious that anything which lessens the discomfort of a situation reduces the incentives to avoid it, and so increases the amount of it. People:

> ... with our lives, in our circles [on North Kensington estates], understand you are better off if you are a single parent. It has reached the point where a lot of people who are not single parents present themselves in that manner because it makes financial sense. If anybody thinks that people like us don't sit around and have these discussions, they are deluding themselves.
>
> We soon figure out which way it will make us the most money. And that is an example of how we are trapped by government policy. Because it discourages us from raising our children in nuclear families ...[3]

As public policy has been formulated in antipathy to the conjugal family, this has been accompanied by (often clearly duplicitous) claims that the state is incapable of influencing family structure or people's living arrangements – despite the ways in which tax/benefit systems are expressly contrived to influence, say, employment, or laws made or altered to prevent anything from robbery to racial discrimination to smoking, and to increase acceptance of, for example, homosexuality. Sometimes, as with the Henshaw report, it is charitable to put this down to naivety.

2   Sir David Henshaw's Report to the Secretary of State for Work and Pensions, *Recovering Child Support: Routes to Responsibility*, Presented to Parliament by the Secretary of State for Work and Pensions, Cm. 6894, 2006.

3   S. Bailey, *No Man's Land: How Britain's inner city young are being failed*, Centre for Young Policy Studies, 2005, p. 21.

The view, mentioned earlier, of people as helpless victims might mean that they are precluded from being responsive to incentives. Is it really being suggested, however, that the poor are somehow different from other people who, we know, do respond to incentives in all sorts of ways? The persistence of determinist perspectives probably makes a contribution to the continued repudiation of any idea that benefit incentives might change behaviour. The emphasis upon inevitability certainly has its *uses* – in case any are tempted to think that matters might be different and responsive to adjustments in the incentives structure. This is one area of research where the present author is aware of considerable self-imposed censorship of unwelcome evidence. Yet sometimes a little light (inadvertently perhaps) creeps through. In a report for the Joseph Rowntree Foundation (no less), the researchers claim that Labour's policies may have increased fertility among low-income families, and that the '... expansion of benefits and tax credits that are assessed against family income with no allowances for the number of adults will reduce the incentive for individuals to cohabit, or to declare cohabitation to the authorities'.[4] Is this not what welfare activists wanted?

A standard response to the question of incentives is that the restructuring and growth of welfare must be seen as a consequence, not a cause, where the increased instability of relationships and upward trend in lone parenthood somehow changed the nature of social security.[5] People's living arrangements are characterised as arising quite spontaneously as individual inventions. As

---

4   M. Brewer and A. Shepherd, *Has Labour Made Work Pay?*, Joseph Rowntree Foundation/Institute of Fiscal Studies, 2004.

5   S. Duncan and R. Edwards (eds), *Single Mothers in an International Context: Mothers or Workers?*, UCL Press, London, 1997.

the jolly jingle has it: families 'come in all shapes and sizes'. In a romping merry-go-round:

> People live in a variety of household types over their lifetime. They may leave their parental home, form partnerships, marry and have children. They may also experience separation and divorce, lone parenthood, and the formation of new partnerships, leading to new households and second families.[6]

People supposedly construct for themselves these multifarious 'alternative family forms', as if 'social institutions evolve in some organic way, just as a language evolves, slowly changing individuals randomly, experimentally modifying existing practices. The law [and the benefits system], like the dictionary, simply registers what has already occurred'.[7] Even if this were so, the question arises of why the trends should have been obediently endorsed and serviced, with no regard for what the consequences might be and whether these might be stalled or reversed. If the incidence of smoking rises, do we provide lighters and ashtrays on buses and hospital wards?

Suggestions that the state has simply rolled over, or been somehow pulled along with the flow, scarcely fit with the hostility directed at marriage, as when writers for the Institute for Public Policy Research continually refer to marriage or support for two-parent families as 'anachronistic'.[8] If policy changes of recent decades have made it increasingly easy for people to live apart and to raise children single-handedly, then

---

6   ONS, 'Households and families', *Social Trends*, 36, 2006.

7   M. Magnet, *The Dream and the Nightmare*, William Morrow, New York, 1993, p. 137.

8   M. Dixon and J. Margo, *Population and Politics*, Institute for Public Policy Research, 2006.

it is difficult to deny that this has been the express intention.

But thinking it does not make it so, and outcome may depart from intention – it often does. In turn, policy-makers may be genuinely unaware of the trade-offs or the unintended consequences of the measures they impose (aside from the fact that they may not care, since they will soon be out of power anyway). Often these people – and/or those who advise them – are disturbingly ignorant. It should be obvious, however, that their intentions or motives, or the declared aims of a programme, are separable from the outcome(s) these might have. Thus, a decision to subsidise participation in the labour market may actually be at the cost of reducing further labour market advancement. This may not be initially appreciated. Giving money to the needy, a seemingly obvious and indisputable way to reduce poverty for those on the left and right alike, may create far more needy people and so on. Whatever the best-laid plans of legislators in Oklahoma in 1999 to increase labour market opportunities for poorer people, they ended up discouraging the stable involvement of men in families, since the greatest financial rewards went to those in unreported cohabitation or living separately.[9]

The prevalence of lone parents has been quite different across the world and over time. Some countries, such as Italy, Japan or Spain, have had low levels, with less than 5 per cent of all families with children headed by a lone parent in the 1990s. There were even decreases. In Italy, they fell 0.54 percentage points between 1991 and 1995, with only 1.7 per cent of women aged 18–60 being lone mothers with a child under eighteen by the mid-1990s. Never-married mothers constituted only 14 per cent of all lone mothers

9   M. Hepner and W. R. Reed, *The Effect of Welfare on Work and Marriage: A View From the States*, Department of Economics, University of Oklahoma, 2004.

(compared with 71 per cent in Denmark). In turn, only 1 per cent of never-married mothers in Italy were cohabiting, compared with 40 per cent in Denmark.

Something must account for this variation. Given an assumption that human beings are utility maximisers, does it not follow that – on balance – young people will have less interest in schooling if they know that social assistance will support them if they leave; that unemployed people will not work, or seek work, if benefits are generous; that some claimants pretend to have illnesses or disabilities in order to get enhanced or more secure benefits? Not only the level but the dependability of benefit income is very important to people's decisions about whether or not to work and, by implication, whether to marry.[10] 'Partners' of the unemployed on income support in the mid-1990s were four times more likely to leave work over a six-month period than were the 'partners' of those receiving non-means-tested unemployment benefit. The former will lose significant amounts of benefit if one person in the household finds a job – the latter will not. Slightly under two-fifths of this lower rate of employment was attributable to the unemployment of the other 'partner', and around a half to the disincentive effects of means-tested benefits.[11]

In the same way, will not lavish benefits supporting lone mothers discourage couples from living together and staying together and facilitate, if not encourage, casual relationships and separation? Pregnancy can lead to housing. Young men can

10 E. Kempson et al., *Hard Times?*, Policy Studies Institute, London, 1994; A. Marsh and S. McKay, *Families, Work and Benefits*, Policy Studies Institute, London, 1993; E. McLaughlin, *Flexibility in Work and Benefits*, Council on Social Justice/Institute for Public Policy Research, London, 1994.

11 S. McKay, R. Walker and R. Youngs, *Unemployment and Jobseeking before Jobseekers Allowance*, DSS Research Report no. 73, Stationery Office, London, 1997.

be sexually feckless if they do not expect to have to support the children they sire. Indeed, a sociobiologist would claim that taking every opportunity to breed when unlimited resources are on tap to sustain your offspring is an evolutionary rooted response and advantage. The babies that a man may accumulate, but does not have to provide for, will depend upon the availability of females who accept the man's children. As people also learn from each other, it is hardly surprising that there are strong associations between having a welfare-dependent birth and the receipt of public assistance by sisters, mothers and other family members.[12]

Far from people not being unresponsive, research on the effects of extra tax credits shows how people even alter their behaviour in response to *anticipated* changes in benefits. An increase in the employment of lone parents with one child anticipated the big rise in in-work benefits after 1999.[13] In the USA, the mass exodus from welfare began before the implementation of the reforms that transformed the system from one of permanent subsidisation to one of temporary assistance. Widespread debate delivered the message that living on welfare was undesirable and that poor people should work, with implied stigmatisation of those who did not.

The factors involved

As with other areas of life, marital and fertility decisions are likely to be influenced by the relative gains and costs someone would experience in changing status, or the expected costs and benefits

---

12   I. Garfinkel and S. McLanahan, *Single Mothers and Their Children: A New American Dilemma*, Urban Institute Press, Washington, DC, 1986.

13   M. Francesconi and W. Van der Klaauw, 'The consequences of "in work" benefit reform in Britain: new evidence from panel data', ISER Working Papers no. 2004-13.

of the different courses open to the individual, and, in William Beveridge's words: 'If money is paid on any condition, it tends to bring that condition about; if it is paid or given on degrading conditions, sooner or later it degrades.'[14] To any economist, the '… penalisation of "virtue" and subsidisation of "vice" (or, in the case of legal aid, criminality) should decrease the supply of the former and increase the supply of the latter, provided that the long-run elasticity of supply is anything greater than the special case of zero, which people seem to implicitly assume when setting up welfare programmes'.[15]

Similarly, if payments in cash and kind raise the welfare available outside the married state by enough, any economic reasons for forming a conjugal household are bound to disappear.[16] That is not to say that, for some or many people, other reasons may not override economic reasons or be concurrent considerations, but it would be foolish to simply assume that people do not change their behaviour in response to the costs and benefits of different directions.

Gary Becker, in his *Treatise on the Family*, characterises the family-formation process as being governed by ways in which men and women evaluate their relative contribution and welfare, and will form couples to the extent that they are reasonably satisfied with their net balance.[17] Marriage depends on its feasibility and desirability, as well as the availability of mates.[18]

14   W. Beveridge, *Voluntary Action: A Report on the Methods of Social Advance*, Allen and Unwin, London, 1948, p. 149.

15   A. Health and D. B. Smith, *At a Price! The True Cost of Public Spending*, Politeia, London, 2006, p. 32.

16   J. Ermisch, 'Familia oeconomica: a survey of the economics of the family', *Scottish Journal of Political Economy*, 40(4), 1993, pp. 353–75.

17   G. S. Becker, *A Treatise on the Family*, Harvard University Press, Cambridge, MA, 1981.

18   R. Dixon, 'Explaining cross-cultural variations in age of marriage and proportion never marrying', *Population Studies*, 25, 1971, pp. 215–33.

Men and woman may choose to marry or not. Women face different choices from men when it comes to children, with different routes into lone motherhood. A woman can have a child without getting married and raise it without the father. Women who expect to get more from marriage will have an incentive not to have a child alone because of the long-term losses involved, unlike women with poorer prospects.[19] Depending on her circumstances, the pay-off for marrying a less desirable man may be less than that of raising a child alone. Whether a woman has an out-of-wedlock child may also depend upon whether and how much the non-resident father (as well as the welfare system) is willing to contribute. Alternatively, a woman can get married, have children and then divorce (as new information about the quality of the match and its alternatives become available).[20]

This may all seem dreadfully unromantic. Where does love or passion fit in? If all were a matter of emotion and spontaneity, however, there would be few patterns or regularities in demographics. There is a tendency to dismiss the role of economics in family-building, as in the Henshaw report, because economic incentives cannot be, or are not, the only factors involved, or because they are more likely to affect decisions at the margins. This is deeply ignorant. The rise of illegitimacy and retreat from marriage may not simply be due to economics, but economics are a large part of the environment in which people make decisions about relationships and children. Getting married – in developed countries, anyway – has historically meant establishing a

---

19   K. Burdett and J. Ermisch, *Single Mothers*, Institute for Social and Economic Research, December 2002.
20   L. Gonzalez, 'The Determinants of the Prevalence of Single Mothers: A Cross Country Analysis', Northwestern University, unpublished, 2003.

new household, which requires sufficient income and reasonably good economic prospects. Unemployment, low wages, insecure jobs and costly housing all provide incentives not to marry and not to have children. At the very least, benefits and exemptions make certain decisions possible which would otherwise have been impossible – that is their point.

Under targeted programmes, 'poor' or 'needy' people are fully compensated for the basic costs of all the children they may produce, unlike those in the broader, middle range of incomes, who have to restrict their childbearing if they are unwilling or unable to absorb the costs involved. Expenditure on children is money that could be spent on alternatives and might have to be, whereas the poor do not have to make choices that involve forgoing one for the other. In the modern world, housing cost and availability have a significant impact on fertility. As it is in competition with children, access to housing is threatened by reproduction, so that higher house prices deter the start of childbearing and the number of children.[21] Women in local authority housing which is responsive to, or increases with, 'need' have always had bigger families. As housing costs have risen, the fertility gap between council tenants and owner-occupiers has increased: by 1986 about a third of owner-occupiers were still childless in their thirties, compared with only 4 per cent in the public sector.[22] At the same time, municipal districts with high concentrations of households in class I (professional and managerial) have long had relatively low illegitimacy ratios, while a majority of births may be out of

21 J. Ermisch,'Economic influences on birth rates', *National Institute Economic Review*, November 1988, pp. 71–81.
22 C. Hakim, *Models of the Family in Modern Society*, Ashgate, 2004.

wedlock where there are largely unskilled populations.[23] Housing paid for by welfare payments is also likely to increase the tendency to live alone, or for people to maximise their property entitlements. US research from the Fragile Families project at Princeton University found that a $150 decrease in the cost of housing was associated with a 36 per cent increase in the likelihood that unwed mothers would live alone.[24]

A person's unearned income reduces their 'need' for earned income, whether their own or someone else's, and non-earned income possessed by women is significantly related to higher fertility.[25] Despite claims to the contrary, international evidence is that generous family allowances encourage early motherhood and bigger families, and that the effect is largest for low-income people.[26] Will the same not apply to welfare? It is almost a tautology that a basic income that is dependent upon reproduction and obviates employment will result in higher birth rates for qualifying women.[27] Unwed childbearing has to be balanced against other available possibilities. Welfare lowers the perceived costs, and the chances of it being adopted will be larger for young, poorly educated and low-ability women whose own personal economic, as well as marital, options are limited.

23 J. Coward, 'Conceptions outside marriage: regional differences', *Population Trends*, 49, 1987; also M. Simms and C. Smith, 'Teenage mothers and their partners: a survey in England and Wales', DHSS Research Report no. 15, HMSO, 1986.

24 Center for Research on Child Well Being, *Housing Policies and Unmarried Mothers' Living Arrangements*, Princeton Working Paper 2006 17-FF.

25 T. P. Schultz, 'Testing the neoclassical model of family labor supply and fertility', *Journal of Human Resources*, XXV(4), pp. 599–626.

26 Ermisch, 'Economic influences on birth rates'.

27 A. Aassve et al., *Employment, Family Union, and Childbearing Decisions in Great Britain*, CASEpaper 84, ESRC Sticerd Toyota Centre, London School of Economics, 2004.

As the researchers for the Policy Studies Institute found, many women who became lone parents 'had worked in low-paid jobs, so life on benefit would not necessarily have entailed a drastic reduction in standard of living'.[28] In the circumstances, exercising the reproductive function is something interesting to do, for which a secure income is provided. Women do not necessarily have children to qualify for benefits, but prior to becoming lone parents they are well aware of their entitlements – not only how 'there would be enough to survive …', but 'how much they could earn within the Income Support disregard, how little they could work and still claim Family Credit …'[29] While they may not plan to conceive, there was 'little sign that the risk of pregnancy concerned them greatly …' They 'would have liked to find a male breadwinner but few seemed to be around' and, given help from benefits, 'the lone parents interviewed felt they no longer needed a man to support them'.[30] For many women, lone motherhood is more desirable than being single without children.

Out-of-wedlock births are overwhelmingly concentrated among women least able to support themselves and their babies. A consistent finding is that women in jobs are about four times more likely to give birth before marriage than those continuing their education, but only half as likely as women in neither further education nor employment.[31] Youngsters with higher opportunity costs, indicated by better grades, higher educational aspirations and higher predicted incomes (for themselves or prospective husbands), expect and desire to marry and have children at older

---

28 K. Rowlingson and S. McKay, *The Growth of Lone Parenthood*, Policy Studies Institute, 1998, p. 199.

29 Ibid., pp. 83 and 159.

30 Ibid., pp. 67 and 199.

31 J. Ermisch, *Lone Parenthood*, Cambridge University Press, Cambridge, 1991.

ages.[32] With good economic prospects, young women have something to lose by having a baby, and are motivated to defer having children, in the same way that the pursuit of living standards has long acted as the great contraceptive of the Western world.[33] Moreover, women with little schooling and low ability also increase their risk of a premarital birth by 2.3 times, or more if their mother had also been a single mother.[34]

It is often suggested that, as women have increased their employment and their economic independence, this has marginalised marriage as an institution in which to rear children, and enabled them to support children on their own. Similar claims are made about how the improved position of married women on the jobs market means that they can 'afford' to leave a marriage. In reality, most separated women, like most unwed mothers, are manifestly not capable of supporting themselves and their children on their own. They are heavily dependent on benefits either in entirety or to supplement earnings. As it is, higher earnings mean more opportunity costs or income forgone by childbearing, rather than additional income *for* childbearing, since women have children and men do not.

32 R. D. Plotnick, *Teenage Expectations and Desires about Family Formation in the United States*, CASEpaper 90, ESRC, Sticerd Toyota Centre, London School of Economics, 2004; and C. J. Duncan and S. D. Hoffman, 'Teenage behavior and subsequent poverty', in C. Jencks and P. E. Peterson (eds), *The Urban Underclass*, Brookings Institution, Washington, DC, 1991.

33 J. B. Hardy and L. S. Zabin, *Adolescent Pregnancy in an Urban Environment: Issues, Programs, and Evaluation*, Urban Institute Press, Washington DC, 1991; R. D. Plotnick, 'The effect of social policies on teenage pregnancy and childbearing', *Families in Society: The Journal of Contemporary Human Services*, 1993, pp. 324–9.

34 E. Del Bono, *Pre-Marital Fertility and Labour Market Opportunities: Evidence from the 1970 British Cohort Study*, Discussion Paper no. 1320, Institute for the Study of Labour, Bonn, 2004; and J. F. Ermisch, *Employment Opportunities and Pre-marital Births in Britain*, ISER, Essex, 2000.

State transfers to the mother also reduce or eliminate the 'cost of fatherhood', however.[35] While some men with low or no earnings may forgo marriage, others may choose instead to father children on women drawn from the lower end of the income distribution who can count on alternative sources of support. Such men may care little about the children produced at zero cost to themselves out of wedlock with various partners. Indeed, since presumptive fatherhood is a proof of masculinity, this gives a man street cred. His voluntary, casual connection to the woman and 'the kid' allows him to maintain the free lifestyle valued by his peer group.

Such feral reproduction is the logical conclusion of the Finer Committee recommendations. No longer are children born into culturally constructed marriage and kinships systems, where parameters are set for the conditions in which young may be produced. Instead, people may randomly reproduce without any resource base of their own, or exercise their democratic rights to enjoy sex and make babies unrestricted by the ability to pay. The 'family' comprises merely the mammalian unit of mother and her offspring, sired by passing males and fed and sheltered by impersonal agencies, who can exercise no constraints on the quality or quantity of children – except perhaps to increase the latter to the degree that they make funding available. The situation is exemplified by the case of Keith Macdonald, a 21-year-old with no qualifications who has already fathered seven children on seven different women. The cost of benefits generated is in the region of £1 million a year.[36]

---

35   R. J. A. Willis, 'Theory of out of wedlock childbearing', *Journal of Political Economy*, 107, 1999, pp. S33–S64.

36   'Seventh baby for father, 21', *Metro*, 3 July 2006.

State of the evidence

It is true that 'compared with the huge body of research on the effect of welfare reforms on marriage and fertility in the USA, this literature is thin indeed in Britain'.[37] The lacuna is related to the way in which lone parenthood, casual relationships and family fragmentation are hardly seen as problematic by the political class or in academia. Opinion in the USA is more mixed, and there has not been so much reticence when it comes to asking questions about the effect of policy on family behaviour.

Most US studies are cross-sectional and rely on interstate variations in benefits to identify welfare effects: an advantage of the USA when formulating academic studies. A prominent disadvantage of such non-longitudinal studies, however, is that little information is provided about the timing of demographic transitions. In turn, studies may also only address one part of the picture. This may be, for example, whether or not women on welfare programmes have a second or further child, but not about the role of welfare in the decision to have the first child.[38] Moreover, the propensity to go on welfare is not quite the same as the role of welfare or other factors in family-building decisions, and effects may not always be in one direction. Care also has to be exercised where there are claims that overall high levels of welfare may mean less family breakdown, if we do not know what kind(s) of welfare is intended or included, and for whom – old people, families generally or other groups?[39]

37 Francesconi and Van der Klaauw, 'The consequences of "in work" benefit reform'.

38 M. R. Rank, 'Fertility among women on welfare: incidence and determinants', *American Sociological Review*, 54, 1989, pp. 296–304.

39 S. L. Zimmerman, 'The welfare state and family breakup: the mythical connection', *Family Relations*, 40, 1991, pp. 139–47.

Welfare benefits and employment

There has been less argument over the issue of welfare dependency per se than there has been about the possible role of benefits in family disruption and fragmentation. It might seem more obvious that an income substitute for employment is, by definition, a discouragement to work – and that the discouragement will be greater the larger the benefit in relation to possible wages.[40] For example, the substantial increase in social assistance benefits in Ontario in the late 1980s has been identified as a major contributor to the doubling of worklessness among lone mothers between 1988 and 1992. Furthermore, while the average stay of a lone parent on welfare was 36 months in 1987, it had become 55 months by 1994.[41] It is rational for dependency to be high, and exits from benefits low, when women have low earning potential, high work expenses or high welfare benefits. So, when exits from benefits occur these will be linked to qualifications, education, the age of children and the level of out-of-work benefits.[42]

A large part of the US cross-state variation in the employment

---

40   Unsurprisingly, 47 per cent of participants in 'Return to Work' programmes run in Britain by the National Council for One Parent Families in the early 1990s said they would be worse off at work and 27 per cent complained of the lack of 'well-paid jobs'. *Lone Parents: Their Potential in the Workforce, NCOPF National Return to Work Programme: A Detailed Report*, National Council for One Parent Families, London, 1993.

41   R. E. Sabatini, *Welfare – No Fair: A Critical Analysis of Ontario's Welfare System* (1985–94), Fraser Institute, Vancouver, 1996; and C. Kapsalis, *Social Assistance Benefit Rates and the Employment Rate of Lone Mothers*, Working Paper no. 2-96-5R, Human Resources Development Canada, Ottawa, 1996.

42   D. T. Ellwood, *Understanding Dependency: Choices, Confidence or Culture?*, Division of Income Security Policy (ISP), US Department of Health and Human Services, 1987; Committee on Ways and Means of the US House of Representatives, *Background Material and Data on Programs within the Jurisdiction of the Committee on Ways and Means*, US Government Printing Office, Washington, DC, 1989, pp. 536–7.

rates of single mothers can be explained by their different demographic characteristics and by the variation in expected income from work compared with out-of-work benefits. Older, more educated mothers are more likely to work while younger mothers or those with numerous children are less likely to be in work. Higher expected returns from working encourage employment.[43] When the cash benefit levels of Aid to Families with Dependent Children (AFDC) fell in real terms in the USA in the 1980s, and eligibility criteria were tightened, the welfare caseload stopped rising for the country as a whole. The rise in employment among lone mothers was, however, much less than the rise in employment of married mothers.

Welfare benefits and childbearing

It has often been claimed that any case for welfare as a cause of female-headed families in the USA – and therefore anywhere else – is null and void because welfare benefits did not retain their value or fell in the USA after 1975 and lone motherhood still went on rising.[44] This does not mean, however, that expanding welfare could not have been part of the cause in the first place.[45] What must be remembered is that US welfare includes food stamps, Medicaid and housing help, which are not always factored into the welfare package in empirical studies. These elements of the welfare

---

43 L. Gonzalez, *Single Mothers and Work*, IZA Bonn Discussion Paper no. 1097, 2004.

44 W. A. Darity and S. L. Myers, 'Family structure and the marginalization of black men: policy implications', in M. B. Tucker and C. Mitchell-Kerman (eds), *The Decline in Marriage among African Americans*, Russell Sage Foundation, New York, 1995.

45 C. Murray, 'How to lie with statistics', *National Review*, 28 February 1986.

package held their value compared with AFDC, and are still available in the aftermath of reform in the mid-1990s which severely restricted entitlements to cash benefits. At very least, it has been quite clear that welfare retards remarriage for divorcees and first marriage for women who have had an out-of-wedlock birth, as well as encouraging girls with babies to set up households apart from their extended families. Irwin Garfinkel and Sarah McLanahan estimated that the increase in welfare benefits accounted for between 9 and 14 per cent of the growth in mother-only families between 1960 and 1975, and for possibly 30 per cent of the growth at the bottom of the income distribution.[46] Other work suggests that half of the increase in US black illegitimacy rates at this time could be attributed to welfare effects in these years of expanding AFDC.[47] In the 1980s, differences in the level of welfare guarantees between states bore a significant, positive relationship with the likelihood of premarital childbearing whether or not considered in relation to factors like the level of unemployment in local labour markets or real per capita income in the state concerned. All the results lead in one direction, even where some researchers find small effects or different effects for whites and blacks.[48]

As it is, the sensitivity of marital status to welfare benefits increased from the late 1960s and into the 1980s (when the real value of AFDC was falling). Stigma and other social controls that inhibited out-of-wedlock childbearing may have declined relative to earlier years – when it is likely that they played a stronger role

46 Garfinkel and McLanahan, *Single Mothers and Their Children*.
47 C. R. Winegarten, 'AFDC and illegitimacy ratios', *Applied Economics*, 20, March 1988, pp. 1589–1601.
48 R. J. Sampson, 'Unemployment and imbalanced sex ratios: race specific consequences for family structure and crime', in Tucker and Mitchell-Kerman, *The Decline in Marriage*.

in damping down any reaction to economic incentives.[49] At this time John Ermisch, using UK data gathered in 1980, concluded that higher welfare benefits raised the proportion of single women who are mothers: specifically, he found that a 10 per cent higher benefit raises the premarital birth rate by 27 per cent.[50]

In the run-up to reform, the US state of New Jersey became the first state to apply a 'family cap', where additional cash benefits were denied for any children born ten or more months after the mother began receiving welfare.[51] The birth rate fell significantly, but disproportionately for black mothers and especially for black mothers living in predominantly white communities. There were also much higher rates of contraceptive use and sterilisation in all groups. Such findings parallel a number of results from other investigations in the USA. Other states also experimented with new approaches to cash assistance for families. Delaware's waiver programme, *A Better Chance*, eliminated all the special rules for two-parent families, applying the same criteria to them as for lone parents, together with increased work requirements and income disregards before benefit could be received. Compared with the situation that pertained under the classic AFDC, there was a large increase in marriage among women under 25 at low educational levels, though there was not an increase in marriage for more educated women. The result was consistent with the findings of similar programmes elsewhere,[52] where there were also increases

49 R. J. Plotnick, 'Welfare and out-of-wedlock childbearing: evidence from the 1980s', *Journal of Marriage and the Family*, 52, 1990, pp. 735–46.

50 Ermisch, *Lone Parenthood*.

51 R. Jagannathan and M. J. Camasso, 'Family cap and nonmarital fertility: the racial conditioning of policy effects', *Journal of Marriage and the Family*, 65, 2003, pp. 52–71.

52 D. Fein, *Will Welfare Reform Influence Marriage and Fertility? Early Evidence from*

in the proportion of recipient families who stayed married.[53] It is also consistent with prior theory – we would not expect significant changes in the behaviour of those women with significant earnings potential and whose net earnings would not be affected by changes in benefits.

The international scene

In addition to the evidence presented above it is also worth highlighting differences in approaches to welfare and differences in outcomes in different countries. One major study – that by Gonzales, discussed below – does, in fact, analyse the influence of benefits on lone parenthood across countries, while controlling for other factors. The other evidence presented below is country-specific.

United Kingdom

The welfare state redistributes from couples with children and multi-person households to single-adult households and older persons. The trend intensified after 1980, and in the late 1990s. The eligible population and the proportion of one-adult households increased rapidly at the same time. More people have come

---

the ABC Demonstration, www.elsevier.com/locate/evalprogplan. Also R. Schoeni and R. Blank, *What Has Welfare Reform Accomplished? Impacts on Welfare Participation, Employment, Income, Poverty and Family Structure*, Working Paper no. 7627, National Bureau of Economic Research, Cambridge, MA, 2000.

53 V. Knox, C. Miller and L. Gennetian, *Reforming Welfare and Rewarding Work: Final Report of the Minnesota Family Investment Program*, MDRC, New York, 2000; see also P. Roberts and M. Greenberg, *Marriage and the TANF Rules: A Discussion Paper*, Center for Law and Social Policy, Washington, DC, 2005.

to live alone and redistribution within households is increasingly less important than it used to be. Instead, more rely on government as a principal or only source of income.

Births outside marriage hovered around 5–6 per cent for much of the nineteenth century and the first half of the twentieth century. Indeed, the illegitimacy rate was remarkably stable for around 400 years (it actually fell to 1 per cent in the mid-seventeenth century).[54] Extraordinary as it now may seem, before and during World War II the illegitimacy rate was actually lower in poor working-class communities and where overall birth rates were at their highest.[55] It probably owes much to the way that, from the 1870s, the establishment of settled communities enabled people to establish networks, not only of support, but surveillance, as respectability became increasingly important to working-class identity.[56] Starting in the 1960s, the proportion of unwed births began to increase, but had barely reached 10 per cent by 1975. By 1980, it had taken off in a cliff-face ascent – rising from 13 per cent to over 30 per cent by 1991, and reaching over 44 per cent in 2003.

If the proportions of women married in each age group had remained at their 1975 values, and the fertility rates of married and unmarried women stayed as they were, then the proportion of births outside marriage would have increased from 9.1 per cent in 1975 to only 11.6 per cent in 2003, rather than the actual

54 J. Ermisch, *An Economic History of Bastardy in England and Wales*, ISER Working Paper 2006-15, and P. Laslett, *Family Life and Illicit Love in Earlier Generations*, Cambridge University Press, Cambridge, 1977.

55 G. Dench, H. Gavron and M. Young, *The New East End*, Profile Books, London, 2006.

56 H. Cook, *The Long Sexual Revolution: English women, sex and contraception, 1800–1975*, Oxford University Press, Oxford, 2004.

2003 level of 44.2 per cent. All this happened at the same time as efficient contraception and abortion became widely available. If the predictions of the sex education and family planning lobby had been borne out, then there should have been a reduction in non-marital fertility rates. As it happened, the advent of the contraceptive pill marks the point at which out-of-wedlock births began to climb slowly, before they exploded upwards after 1980. Benefits for lone mothers, however, became more available and much more generous as, at the same time, men's sexual access to women was less contingent upon marriage. Women's ability to control their fertility, and the emphasis on their exclusive rights to decide whether or not to carry a pregnancy to term, may itself have weakened any sense of responsibility for a pregnancy or obligation towards a pregnant girlfriend. As marriage received less favourable treatment, the number of babies born to married couples halved over 30 years. Are changes to taxation and welfare part of the explanation?

One thing that is certain is the '… statistical fact: the sudden enormous increase in never-married mothers coincided with changes in the social welfare structure which rewarded that group preferentially over married couples'.[57]

From a slightly different angle, a fertility decline for UK lone mothers with one child has been observed as wages were boosted (via in-work benefits) in the late 1990s, leading to increased employment. Limits on the number of children that can benefit from childcare support may also have increased the inconvenience of having more children for more employable women.[58] But

---

57 'Facts and fatherhood', Leader, *The Times*, 10 November 1993.
58 Francesconi and Van der Klaauw, 'The consequences of "in work" benefit reform'.

these changes that increased benefits did, of course, simultaneously increase the loss of benefit from couple formation. Over the
same period there was a big drop (25 per cent) in annual (official)
'partnering' rates.

Australia

Other Anglophone countries have seen similar developments.
As their tax and benefit systems were overhauled from ones
of universal family support to become targeted on the 'needy'
– especially in the 1980s – welfare dependency and lone parenthood rocketed upwards. Australian ex-nuptial births rose from
9.7 per cent of births in the year before the introduction of the
Sole Parent Benefit (SPB, replacing ad hoc state and charity provision) to 14.7 per cent in the following year, and the numbers
receiving SPB rose fivefold over the 1980s. By 1997, the proportion of ex-nuptial births was 27 per cent, and the nuptial birth rate
had nearly halved.[59] More than three-quarters of the increase in
jobless families, which happened at that time, was because of the
explosive increase in sole parents. As with prior divorce legislation in the UK, the feasibility of the 1975 Family Law Act rested
upon the availability of state support for lone parents, and this
rapidly turned from a minor to a major component of the welfare
bill. Women with feminist agendas operating in bureaucratic and
government circles played 'a central role in defining their needs
and in influencing social policy …' so that the state came to '…
provide the income maintenance that they needed to achieve
independence. Their right to have a family without a husband had

59 L. Sullivan, *Behavioural Poverty*, Policy Monographs no. 45, Centre for Independent Studies, St Leonards, NSW, 2000.

been given public recognition'.[60] By the century's end, more than 20 per cent of the non-aged population depended on welfare for most of their income, and almost half of less educated, low-ability and unwed women were now lone mothers.

New Zealand

Much the same applies to New Zealand. Only 2–3 per cent of working-age adults were dependent on social security benefits as their primary source of income 30 years ago. A system of universal acknowledgement for family dependents by the tax system was then replaced by a welfare system targeting the needy. One in four families became a sole parent during the 1980s and one in five families had a sole parent supported by welfare. The increase in Domestic Purposes Benefit (DPB) recipients accounts for the greater part of the increase in numbers of sole parents.[61] With no fiscal recognition *at all* for two-parent families above a low income level, sole parents essentially became the only recognised family type in New Zealand. The proportion of lone parents collecting the DPB had peaked at nearly 90 per cent by 1991. Extraordinarily, the number of male recipients rose by nearly 500 per cent.

In a process that parallels the earlier experience of American

60   S. Swain and R. Howe, *Single Mothers and Their Children: Disposal, Punishment and Survival in Australia*, Cambridge University Press, Cambridge, 1995, p. 206; M. McHugh and J. Millar, 'Single mothers in Australia: supporting mothers to seek work', in S. Duncan and R. Edwards, *Single Mothers in an International Context: Mothers or Workers?*, UCL Press, London, 1997.

61   M. Rochford, 'A profile of sole parents from the 1991 census', Research Report Series no. 15, Social Policy Agency Research Unit, 1993; D. A. Preston, 'Welfare benefit reform', *Social Policy Journal of New Zealand*, 8, March 1997, pp. 29–36; and see P. Morgan, *Family Matters: Family Breakdown and Its Consequences*, New Zealand Business Roundtable, Wellington, 2004.

blacks, two-parent families have virtually vanished among Maori, when these were overwhelmingly the norm in the mid-twentieth century. The effective absorption of formal marriage into cohabitation in 2002, as both relationships were given identical legal status, was followed by a further and sudden slump in marriages.

USA

In the USA, the pattern of growth in the Aid to Families with Dependent Children (AFDC) caseload corresponds closely to the change in the level and availability of the benefit. This created a structure where it was significantly more difficult for two-parent families than lone parent families to receive assistance; in which family benefits were sharply reduced or eliminated if an AFDC mother married her children's father or brought a step-parent into the household; and where families would lose assistance if there was any wage earner in the home.[62] Between 1963 and 1972 the average real benefit (for a family of four) increased by 35 per cent, and Medicaid, housing, school meals, food stamps and other resources added to the welfare package. The percentage of female-headed families going on the AFDC programme increased from 29 per cent to 63 per cent. As AFDC levels and welfare participation rose together, there was also a 50 per cent rise in the number of female-headed families. From the records, June O'Neill calculated that a 50 per cent increase in monthly AFDC and food stamps would be likely to precipitate a 75 per cent increase in both the

62 Ronald Reagan referred to this problem at length in his acclaimed 1964 speech 'A time for choosing'. He quoted a judge who telephoned him about women who were filing for divorce specifically to raise their net income. The speech can be downloaded both in text and sound file form from: http://millercenter.virginia. edu/scripps/diglibrary/prezspeeches/reagan/index.html.

numbers of women enrolled on the programme and the number of years spent on AFDC, together with a 43 per cent increase in out-of-wedlock births.[63] There was also less pressure on young men to get work as the necessity to support a family fell.

Previous evidence suggests that US states that permitted poor married fathers to obtain welfare (under a scheme called AFDC-UP) had higher marriage rates than did states where help was limited to poor mothers.[64] This may be double edged, however, since the US Panel Study of Income Dynamics[65] suggests that couples who received means-tested relief in the previous year were more likely to separate than those who did not, presumably because this exposed people to the potential of the benefits system at the same time as the man's poor economic position was highlighted. Husbands' low earnings particularly encouraged separation when wives had no earnings.[66] Separation fell when the wife acquired some earnings (the odds of separation associated with a $10,000 decline in husband's earnings were four times larger when the wife had no earnings than when she had earnings). This may have prevented marital dissolution in the US context by extending the couple's combined income. Low or no-husband earnings may be more disruptive when the wife has no earnings since it is then that prospective benefit income looks most attractive.

63 M. A. Hill and J. O'Neill, *Underclass Behavior in the United States: Measurement and Analysis of Determinants*, Baruch College, City University of New York, 1993.

64 R. Moffitt, 'Incentive effects of the US welfare system: a review', *Journal of Economic Literature*, 30, 1992, pp. 1–61.

65 H. Ono, 'Husbands and wives' resources and marital dissolution', *Journal of Marriage and the Family*, 60, 1998, pp. 674–89.

66 Ibid.

France

Contemporary France has a lower rate of lone motherhood than the UK. The percentage of births outside marriage is similar, but many are to cohabiting couples who tend to marry or maintain longer relationships than their counterparts in the UK. A specific benefit for lone mothers is available only for a year after separation or until the youngest child is three years old. Lone parents are then expected to work. Those that do not are eligible for social assistance, provided at subsistence level. Housing benefits are not generous. While lone parents experience a significant drop in living standards after housing costs are considered, lone parenthood is not associated with poverty as much as in the UK. Lone parents are far more likely to work full time and a half 'repartner' within five years.[67]

Italy

In Italy, the real value of family allowances actually decreased by 38 per cent between 1988 and 1994: lone-parent families did not receive any supplements, and there has been generally weak support for anyone with children or in the working-age population. Family and kin are assumed to provide help outside the labour market, and the welfare state has a bias towards helping employed and elderly people. The level of assistance was actually lower for one-parent families compared with two-parent families – an unusual occurrence among modern benefits systems – and lone-parent families actually declined for a while (see above),

---

67   R. O'Neill, *Fiscal Policy and the Family: How the family fares in France, Germany and the UK*, Institute for the Study of Civil Society, London, 2005.

albeit from a low level anyway.[68] This is now slowly changing under pressure from the EU and concerns over very low overall birthrates.

Wider international comparisons

Studies of the determinants of lone parenthood have been primarily limited to single countries. Libertad Gonzalez, however, used data from seventeen countries, where there may be large variation in wages, benefit levels and institutional settings, to examine the international trends in lone motherhood during the 1980s and 1990s.[69] Findings are that increases in the level of public support for lone mothers have been significantly and positively associated with a higher prevalence of both never-married and divorced mothers. Previous findings using more limited variables also indicated that higher benefit levels were generally associated with higher levels of lone parenthood, with a clear progression from countries like Greece, Spain and Italy (with very low rates for both) up to Denmark.[70] As might be predicted, an increase in benefits for lone parents that leaves constant the benefits for other types of families has a stronger effect, compared with an increase in benefits for all types of families. The level of male earnings had more significant effects on the prevalence of never-married mothers than on the prevalence of divorced mothers. An overall increase in average male earnings of, for example, 10 per cent decreased the prevalence of

68 P. Morgan, *Family Policy: Family Changes. Italy, Sweden and the UK compared*, Institute for the Study of Civil Society, 2006.

69 Gonzalez, *The Determinants of the Prevalence of Single Mothers*.

70 P. Whiteford and J. Bradshaw, 'Benefits and incentives for lone parents: a comparative analysis', *International Social Security Review*, 47, 1994, pp. 69–89.

lone mothers by 1.3 percentage points (from, say, 6 per cent to 4.7 per cent of all women).

Pursuing the subject further, Gonzalez used household panel data from an eight-year period (1994–2001) for women aged 18–35 likely to be most affected by labour market conditions and benefit levels, and found a high correlation between benefit levels and the incidence of single mothers. The UK was the country with both the highest incidence of single motherhood and the highest benefit levels in 2001. Controlling for age, education, male wages and unemployment rates still left countries with yearly benefits 1,000 euros above the European average with about 17 per cent more single mothers than those with an average level of benefits, and with an incidence of single headship about 15 per cent higher. Further attempts to control for the level of a country's tolerance of these types of families still left a direct economic impact, so that 1,000 euros above average is associated with a 2 per cent increase in the likelihood that a woman will become a single mother, with a far greater impact on those with low education levels.[71] This 'tolerance' of lone mothers may itself be, in large part, a consequence of favouritism in the benefits system (see below).

Labour market influences on lone parenthood

Any choice of model suggests that if one economic factor is important, others are likely to be so as well: one cannot simply focus on benefits to lone parents compared with parents in a relationship.[72]

---

71 L. Gonzalez, *The Effect of Benefits on Single Motherhood in Europe*, Discussion Paper 2026, IZA, Bonn, 2006.

72 D. T. Ellwood, *Understanding Dependency*, US Department of Health and Human Services, Washington, DC, 1987, p. 90.

Factors like the ease or difficulty of finding a spouse with stable employment, or rising or falling levels of male earnings, are bound to confound predictions based on welfare alone. Many demographic and labour market decisions are made simultaneously or jointly and are therefore interlinked,[73] hence the interrelationship between leaving home, union formation, childbearing, employment and educational choice.

In one historical period a certain factor or combination of factors may be important, but then become less so in another. A problem with all research is that it is time-specific. Family behaviour is subject to a variety of influences that individually may assume greater or lesser importance under given circumstances at different times and may interact with each other. One analysis of US teenagers' desires and expectations about marriage, childbearing and becoming unwed parents found that family context (race, ethnicity, sex, type of religious upbringing, parental education and parental expectations about education), and social psychological perspectives, all had predictive power.[74]

Few studies address the relationship between numerous variables. Men's economic fortunes have always been an important factor driving demographic change, with statistical links between wars and trade cycles and marriage rates.[75] Also, where there is a relative oversupply of women (low sex ratio), men will not only be

73 Aassve et al., *Employment, Family Union, and Childbearing Decisions in Great Britain*.

74 R. D. Plotnick, *Teenage Expectations and Desires about Family Formation in the United States*, CASEpaper 90, ESRC Sticerd Toyota Centre, London School of Economics, 2004.

75 V. A. Oppenheimer, 'A theory of marriage timing', *American Journal of Sociology*, 94, 1988, pp. 563–91.

less inclined to marry (since they have more options) but, if they do, they may be less committed. Even higher-income men will be less inclined to marry and more likely to develop weak commitments where there is a perceived 'excess' of women.

A pool of securely employed males is usually necessary for any viable marriage market. Most people define the male parenting role to include being the main provider, even if few would now support the view that employment is a male prerogative. A man's earnings tend to be regarded in terms of a 'family wage', even when rates of pay and conditions of employment may not provide an income that is reliable and large enough to meet household needs. Male employment is still an important part of a consistently demonstrable and direct relationship between the timing of marriage, marital stability and economic conditions, and has substantial effects on marriage rates and birth patterns. Male employment and earnings facilitate marriage and marital births; female employment and earnings act as a barrier. While poorer employment opportunities for young women reduce the woman's opportunity costs of childbearing, and thereby indirectly increase childbearing, poor employment opportunities for young men discourage marriage, thereby increasing the population of young women at risk of having a birth outside marriage and making it more likely that a pregnant women does not marry the father of the child. Increases in the wages of women relative to men are generally associated with fertility reduction and with a reallocation of women's time from non-market to market work. In contrast, increases in the labour productivity and wages of men can enhance the attractions of a larger family and are associated with higher levels of fertility.

Historically, higher male unemployment discouraged

marriage and increased non-marital births among pregnant brides-to-be, with a recovery in marriages in subsequent years. As poorer people are most affected by changes in labour market conditions, and because a smaller fall in productivity can push the wages of poorer people below subsistence or benefit levels, non-marital childbearing is usually found disproportionately in the lower socio-economic levels of society and has been found to be as far back as Tudor times.[76] The exception to this was in the interwar years, when the marriages of single women were affected by higher unemployment and birth rates generally fell, but illegitimacy did not rise. Fewer women may have become pregnant in the lead-up to marriage owing to the culture of sexual restraint that was at its peak in these years.[77]

Since men are less desirable as spouses if they do not have a 'decent' job,[78] not only may desertion and marital disruption be linked to the inability of fathers to reliably provide for their families, but out-of-wedlock childbearing may be more prevalent when females are not only in excess supply, but where the gains to marriage are small because male incomes are low or unstable:[79]

> couples rarely chance marriage unless a man has a job; often the job is temporary, low paying, insecure, and the worker gets laid off whenever he is not needed. Women come to realise that welfare benefits and ties within kin

76 P. Slack, *Poverty and Policy in Tudor and Stuart England*, Longman, London, 1988.

77 Ermisch, *An Economic History of Bastardy in England and Wales*.

78 T. M. Cooney and D. P. Hogan, 'Marriage in an institutionalised life course: first marriage among American men in the twentieth century', *Journal of Marriage and the Family*, 53, 1991, pp. 176–90.

79 R. A. Easterlin, *Birth and Fortune: The impact of numbers on personal welfare*, Basic Books, New York, 1980.

networks provide greater security for them and their children.[80]

The worst economic profiles are found for men who have neither married nor cohabited more than sporadically with the mothers of their children.[81] Women are particularly likely to consider marriage when the man earns more than some minimum threshold, something that is relatively resistant to change in the face of fluctuating labour market prospects.[82] In eleven out of fourteen major studies, findings were that men with higher education, higher earnings, greater labour force attachment, and so on, were more likely to marry. Of the six studies that included the characteristics of both men and women, two found effects for the economic characteristics of men but not women, four for both, and none found effects for women alone.[83]

Long-term decline in the MMPI (Marriageable Male Pool Index) as an important contributor to family disruption and the rise in lone-mother families was first demonstrated in American black communities. With post-industrial economic transforma-

---

80 C. Stack, *All Our Kin; Strategies for Survival in a Black Community*, Harper and Row, New York, 1974, p. 113.

81 M. Maclean and J. Eekelaar, *The Parental Obligation*, Hart, Oxford, 1997, p. 143, and S. Speak, S. Cameron and R. Gilroy, *Young Single Fathers*, Family Policies Study Centre, London, 1997.

82 G. J. Duncan and S. D. Hoffman, 'Teenage underclass behaviour and subsequent poverty: have the rules changed?', in Jencks and Peterson, *The Urban Underclass*.

83 P. J. Smock, W. D. Manning and M. Porter, '"Everything's there except money": how economic factors shape the decision to marry among cohabiting couples', *Journal of Marriage and the Family*, 67, 2005, pp. 680–96; see also S. Sassler and R. Schoen, 'The effects of attitudes and economic activity on marriage', *Journal of Marriage and the Family*, 61, 1999, pp. 147–59, and Y. Xie et al., 'Economic potential and entry into marriage and cohabitation', *Demography*, 40, 2003, pp. 351–67.

tion under way, employment and marriage both fell gradually in the 1960s, then rapidly in the 1970s and 1980s. As the probability of marriage declined for black women, there was a growing excess of women over men in every age group in the marriageable years. From the 1960s, successively smaller cohorts of black men and fathers have been stably employed, depending instead on informal and government assistance or illicit activities.[84]

The pool of employed men with adequate earnings has repeatedly accounted for more of the racial difference in US marriage rates than any other variable.[85] This alone cannot explain the drastic marital decline but, at the lowest estimate, about 20 per cent of the changes in marriage rates for US blacks from 1960 to 1980 are attributable to decreasing employment among that group.[86] It is certainly not a reason to dismiss the role of welfare (or anything else), even given that the rates of cash benefits fell after 1975, since the returns from other options may have been falling even faster. Moreover, in examining the relationship between labour market prospects and marriage, it should not be

---

84   W. J. Wilson and K. Neckerman, 'Poverty and family structure: the widening gap between evidence and public policy issues', in S. H. Danziger and D. H. Weinberg (eds), *Fighting Poverty: What Works and What Doesn't*, Harvard University Press, Cambridge, MA, 1986; D. T. Lichter, F. B. LeClere and D. K. McLaughlin, 'Local marriage markets and the marital behaviour of black and white women', *American Journal of Sociology*, 96, 1991, pp. 843–67; A. J. Cherlin, *Marriage, Divorce, Remarriage*, Harvard University Press, Cambridge, MA, 1981; M. Testa et al., 'Employment and marriage among inner city fathers', *Annals of the American Academy of Political and Social Science*, 501, 1989, pp. 79–91.

85   D. T. Lichter, D. K. McLaughlin, G. Kephart and D. J. Landry, 'Race and the retreat from marriage: a shortage of marriageable men?', *American Sociological Review*, 57, 1992, pp. 781–99; Lichter et al., 'Local marriage markets'; and S. J. South and K. M. Lloyd, 'Marriage opportunities and family formation: further implications of imbalanced sex ratios', *Journal of Marriage and the Family*, 54, 1992, pp. 440–51.

86   R. D. Mare and C. Winship, 'Socioeconomic change and the decline of marriage for blacks and whites', in Jencks and Peterson, *The Urban Underclass*.

forgotten that benefits themselves affect the extent of attachment to the labour market itself.

The male factor

Both the number of men (a demographic dimension) and their employment (a socio-economic dimension) have significant independent effects on family variables. Relationships between sex ratios and marriage and divorce persist despite controlling for age, education, income and other personal attributes. Areas studies show, for example, how the sex ratio alone has strong effects on the percentage of women who are married; the rate of marital births per thousand women; the percentage of husband-and-wife families; the percentage of children living in couple families; and the increase in unwed births.[87] Altogether, the lower the sex ratio and the lower the male employment rate the higher the rate of female-headed families with children and the percentage of single women.[88] Economic recessions may account for about a third of the overall increase in US mother-only families between 1968 and 1988.[89]

---

87 K. J. Kiecolt and M. A. Fossett, 'Mate availability and marriage among Africa Americans: aggregate and individual level analyses', in Tucker and Mitchell-Kerman, *The Decline in Marriage*.

88 R. J. Sampson, 'Unemployment and imbalanced sex ratios: race specific consequences for family structure and crime', in Tucker and Mitchell-Kerman, *The Decline in Marriage*; M. Testa and M. Krogh, 'The effect of employment on marriage among black males in inner-city Chicago', in ibid; and Testa et al., 'Employment and marriage among inner city fathers'. Some results show more effects on marriage rates than on lone parenthood. See also South and Lloyd, 'Marriage opportunities and family formation', and R. D. Plotnick, 'Determinants of out-of-wedlock childbearing: evidence from the National Survey of Youth' (mimeo), School of Social Work, University of Washington, Seattle, 1988.

89 D. J. Hernandez, *America's Children: Resources from Family, Government, and the Economy*, Russell Sage Foundation, New York, 1993.

Male behaviour in response to high unemployment must be seen in the context of domestic 'deregulation', where men's status in the community is uncoupled from the performance of family duties. Over time, successively larger proportions of fathers are unmarried at the conception and birth of their first child. In US studies from the 1960s, couples who faced a premarital pregnancy tended to marry earlier than those who did not. The social pressures to legitimise the birth often outweighed financial concerns while, more recently, declining stigma, the availability of welfare benefits and the mother's access to other support may have diluted the pressure to conform.[90] These processes become self-reinforcing, since declining marriage itself promotes poor male employment and earnings and, consequently, falling marriage-ability. Cultural transmission, or the lack of it, means that, as lone parenthood is passed on down generations, the ability to earn a decent living as much as the expectation of working consistently, and the way to conduct a marital relationship, all get lost because the scripts disappear.[91]

On this side of the Atlantic, individual-level studies of family dissolution, analyses of trends over time, as well as census, or cross-sectional, data, all show a strong connection between employment and income and divorce and marriage.[92] In the

90 W. A. Darity and S. L. Myers, 'Family structure and the marginalization of black men: policy implications', in Tucker and Mitchell-Kerman, *The Decline in Marriage*.

91 K. S. Hymowitz, 'Dads in the 'hood', *City Journal*, August 2004.

92 J. Haskey, 'Social class and socio-economic differentials in divorce in England and Wales', *Population Studies*, 38(3), 1984, pp. 419–38; R. Lampard, 'An examination of the relationship between marital dissolution and unemployment', Working Paper 17, Social Change and Economic Life Institute, 1990; M. J. Murphy, 'Demographic and socio-economic influence on recent British marital breakdown patterns', *Population Studies*, 39(3), 1985. See also S. Cameron, 'A review of economic

Policy Studies Institute investigation of the growth of lone parent-hood, couples were three times more likely to separate if the man was unemployed,[93] and twice as likely in the British Household Panel Study (1991–97).[94] Upon examination of the unemployment variation over time in 300 areas, findings were that a one percentage point higher local unemployment rate increased the annual probability of a woman having a premarital birth by about 0.4 percentage points, which represents a 10 per cent increase in the premarital first birth rate (and a 2–3 per cent increase in the overall rate by age 27).[95] In the 1970 cohort study data, local male unemployment rates were also positively and significantly related to out-of-wedlock births and negatively to union formation.[96]

Not only may the economic contribution of males with low earning potential be unacceptably low, but their prospects may also be poor. Indeed, the weak economic position of the young father provides a strong link between premarital pregnancy and the breakdown rates of subsequent marriages.[97] Those able to improve their economic position have noticeably higher marital

---

research into determinants of divorce', *British Review of Economic Issues*, 17(41), 1995, pp. 1–22.

93 K. Rowlingson and S. McKay, *The Growth of Lone Parenthood*, Policy Studies Institute, London, 1998.

94 R. Böheim and J. Ermisch, 'Breaking up: financial surprises and partnership', Paper presented at the Royal Economic Society Conference , Nottingham, 1999; J. Ermisch, 'Cohabitation and childrearing outside marriage in Britain', in L. Wu and B. Wolfe (eds), *Out of Wedlock: Causes and Consequences of Nonmarital Fertility*, Russell Sage Foundation, New York, 2002.

95 Ermisch, *Employment Opportunities and Pre-marital Births*.

96 Del Bono, *Pre-marital Fertility and Labour Market Opportunities*.

97 See F. F. Fustenberg, Jr, 'Premarital pregnancy and marital stability', in Levinger and Moles, *Divorce and Separation*, Basic Books, New York, 1979, and K. E. Kiernan, 'Teenage marriage and marital breakdown: a longitudinal study', *Population Studies*, 40(1), 1986, pp. 35–54.

stability as higher earnings by the husband reduce the possibility of dissolution.[98] In turn, the association between low divorce proneness and high husband education tends to disappear once income level is considered, as do occupational differences. The associations are worldwide. German husbands' unemployment significantly increases the risk of separation in the following year, and the impact increases with duration of unemployment.[99] The same is true for Sweden. So firm is the connection that any academic dispute is over the relative importance of the financial and the social-psychological factors associated with unemployment, not its connection to separation.[100]

From this plethora of research we may conclude that the lessening ability of men (particularly less skilled and educated men) to make sufficient and stable provision for families may have had an important influence in fostering high rates of non-marriage, family breakdown and children without fathers throughout the Anglophone world. It provides further evidence that economic considerations do affect the decision to marry and to stay married. It is worth adding that not all the effects of variables such as unemployment arise directly from economic considerations.

Studies from the USA of non-marital fertility which include labour market variables (employment and/or income) find the most significant relationships between unwed motherhood and

98   S. D. Hoffman and G. J. Duncan, 'The effect of incomes, wages, and AFDC benefits on marital disruption', *Journal of Human Resources*, XXX(1), pp. 19–41.

99   K. Kraft, 'Unemployment and the separation of couples', *KYKLOS*, 54(1), 2001, pp. 67–88.

100 K. K. Charles and M. Stephens, 'Job displacement, disability, and divorce', *Journal of Labour Economics*, 22(2), 2004, and J. L. Starkey, 'Race differences in the effect of unemployment on marital instability: a socioeconomic analysis', *Journal of Socio-Economics*, 25(6), 1996, pp. 683–720.

welfare levels, particularly when it is male earning opportunities and thus women's potential resources from marriage which are juxtaposed with welfare. In the USA between 1960 and 1980, illegitimacy was low when both market wages and the probability of earning these wages were high relative to the level of welfare benefits, and vice versa.[101]

The fact that men with higher incomes are more likely to marry, and better-off families are more likely to stay together, makes family structure a consequence of as well as a cause of poverty (however evaluated).[102] Between the mid-1970s and the mid-1990s, there was a doubling in the proportion of low-paid men in the UK. Unfortunately, it is male *employment* which attracts attention in the UK – as something to condemn as threatening to family life.

Summary

The evidence is clear from cross-sectional and longitudinal studies that economic incentives do matter when people take family decisions, which is not to say that other factors are not sometimes important. The direct relationships between the tax and benefits systems and family circumstances are clearly important. Also important are the levels of rewards and security of employment – especially to the lower-paid. These variables, particularly the latter, will themselves be influenced by the level of benefits, but there will be other, independent, factors that will influence such

---

101 M. S. Bernstam and P. L. Swan, *The State as Marriage Partner of Last Resort: A Labour Market Approach to Illegitimacy in the United States, 1960–1980*, Australian School of Management Working Paper 86-029, Kensington, 1986.

102 M. J. Bane, 'Household composition and poverty', in Danziger and Weinberg, *Fighting Poverty*.

labour market conditions, including the labour supply. In the past, weak labour market conditions tended to lead to a reduction in marriages and births rather than to an increase in lone parents. Looking at the evidence as a whole, today's benefits system can be seen as underwriting a decision to have children looked after by a lone parent when the earning potential of the father is relatively weak. Potentially, the benefits system has three effects. First, it can encourage lone parenthood rather than couple formation because of the bias in tax and benefits systems against couples – particularly single-earner couples. Second, it can encourage childbearing as opposed to a decision not to have children. Third, the benefits system can, itself, bring about labour market conditions that are less conducive to couples taking a decision to marry.

5   RHETORIC AND REALITY

The phoney war on lone parents

The possibility of a connection between subsidies and family fragmentation is often dismissed because the sharpest increase in out-of-wedlock births and lone parenthood was in the times and aftermath of the premiership of Margaret Thatcher, who, we are repeatedly told, decimated the welfare system. Such claims are projections rooted in left-wing enmity, and they do not stand up to scrutiny. In her time, welfare spending was expressly targeted the 'needy' and parents who were not on welfare saw their fiscal supports eroded and charges imposed on mutuality. The justif- ications for and debates on the community charge or poll tax, in and outside of Parliament, were explicitly hostile to couple and multi-person households. Meanwhile, One Parent Benefit (a non- means-tested payment) was increased. In John Major's time, when Chancellor Kenneth Clarke spoke of an 'anomaly' he meant the tax allowance for married couples, not lone parent benefits.

The years 1979 to 1992 were also the times when benefit dependency dramatically increased, the number of working lone parents declined, and lone parenthood became a mass phenom- enon.[1] While the base rates of income support were largely

---

1   P. Bingley, E. Symons and I. Walker, 'Child support, income support and lone mothers', *Fiscal Studies*, 15(1), 1994, pp. 81–98.

unchanged, apart from rises in child additions, recipients now had considerable help with housing costs, which soared over this period. The real net income to which the non-employed were entitled rose substantially compared with that received by those in work – with a real increase of 47 per cent (nearly half of which occurred between 1981 and 1984). The large rise in unemployment in the late 1970s and early 1980s coincided with the tendency to protect non-working parents from the tribulations of the housing and labour markets at a time that also saw the emphatic rejection of family policy, or universal recognition for the costs of child rearing. The massive losses of traditional male jobs must be seen in relation to the evidence that exposure to means-tested relief when men are in a precarious economic position encourages separation, as much as non-marriage. The evidence for the USA quoted earlier is paralleled by that from the British Household Panel Study, where receipt of income support raised disruption rates nearly fourfold.[2]

Tax and benefit changes in the Conservative years did not so much favour 'traditional' nuclear families – the standard accusation – but, in a rather more accurate take on 'new state libertarianism' by other critics, this was 'not a withdrawal of interference in private lives as much as the exercise of a new set of rules privileging a powerful interest group' (of two career couples) and 'a growing entourage of fellow-travelling adult "singles" … similarly promoted by fiscal policies treating family life as a lifestyle choice'.[3]

2   R. Böheim and J. Ermisch, 'Breaking up: financial surprises and partnership', Paper presented at the Royal Economic Society Conference, Nottingham, 1999.

3   G. Dench, *Rediscovering Family*, Hera Trust, 2003. pp. 51 and 54.

Changing the climate

As economic imperatives made children increasingly incompatible with marriage from the late 1970s onwards, a bifurcated family pattern took shape wherein more affluent families postponed or renounced childbearing, while the subsidised poor did not. The subsequent assault on child poverty from 1997 increased the amount of state support that is contingent upon having children for no-income and low-income people – support that is far higher for lone than for couple parents. Changes in the drivers or determinants of non-marital childbearing – such as the rise in unemployment combined with the enhancement of welfare in the early 1980s – not only directly raised the level but also likely eroded the stigma. By rewarding some behaviours and penalising others, tax and welfare systems affect the preference and behaviour of individuals not just through hard cash calculations but by (unavoidably) embodying and promoting certain values and assumptions. In other words, they send out messages, where something that pays a penalty is perceived as unworthy and that which receives a bonus is to be approved and emulated. The generous subsidisation of the lone-parent household cannot but reinforce the belief that it is quite acceptable for men to expect the state to provide for their offspring. The withdrawal of tax allowances to married couples sends out the message that this relationship is not valued. As observed by a retiring president of the Family Division of the High Court, the absence of a 'financial incentive to marry or remain married and a financial incentive to cohabit and not to marry … contributes to the downgrading of the status of marriage …'[4] The process, like any other, is also self-endorsing and perpetu-

4   Dame E. Butler-Sloss, 'Family law reform – opportunities taken, wasted and yet to be seized', Lecture to the Bar Council, 5 December 2005.

ating, with the resulting increasing prevalence of lone mother-hood in the population, the spread of cohabitation and decline in marriages.

It can be argued that such changes in norms which favour or tolerate lone motherhood lead to further changes to the benefit system in favour of lone mothers. Here we need to remind ourselves how Libertad Gonzalez identified a direct effect of benefits on lone motherhood and an effect for the level of a country's tolerance of these types of families.[5] John Ermisch identifies a self-reinforcing rise in childbearing outside marriage,[6] whereby changes in the economic climate that alter non-marital child-bearing behaviour produce further dramatic and ongoing change through the social influences that make this an acceptable, even preferred, way to have families, so that the more lone parenthood there is, the more lone parenthood there will be. Similarly, the fall in the married population and thus marital births through the dramatic rise in cohabitation (see below), once kick-started, becomes the accepted way to conduct sexual relationships.

Even so, hard economics tends to hold a trump card. It needs to be borne in mind that attitudes also changed to favour lone motherhood among higher-income groups, but it is in lower-income groups (those most directly affected by the benefit system) that this has increased so dramatically. Significantly, the dynamic is concentrated among the section of the population that has the most direct incentives to raise children as lone parents.

---

5   L. Gonzalez, *The Effect of Benefits on Single Motherhood in Europe*, Discussion Paper 2026, IZA, Bonn, 2006.

6   J. Ermisch, *An Economic History of Bastardy in England and Wales*, ISER Working Paper 2006-15.

Liability for child support

Does child support liability lower the incentives for fathers to separate or raise incentives for mothers? Evidence from the USA is that more strict enforcement of child support lowers unwed births[7] and, if child support is calculated on non-custodial parental income, rather than on a couple's aggregate income, child support liability reduces separation rates. Strengthening child support enforcement not only leads men to have fewer out-of-wedlock births, but they seem to become choosier about whom they have them with. When child support enforcement is strengthened, it seems to have the effect of leading men to select mothers of higher ability, who may better care for and invest in their children as, at the same time, they sire fewer children.[8]

From the British Household Panel Study of couples with dependent children during the 1990s, findings are that the mandatory child support had an unintended impact on the separation rate: reducing the probability of separation by 20 per cent if liability on the non-custodial parent was enforced. Reforms that reduced fathers' liabilities were predicted to reverse this tendency and increase separation by, on average, about 10 per cent above the contemporary level.

Sir David Henshaw's report to the Secretary of State for Work and Pensions, *Recovering Child Support*, appears to be oblivious to these findings. Not only have non-resident fathers had to (formally) pay progressively less in the UK, with little attempt

---

7   E. Gaylinsky, S. McLanahan and I. Garfinkel, *Will Child Support Enforcement Reduce Nonmarital Childbearing?*, Paper presented at the annual meeting of the Population Association of America, Washington, DC, 1997.

8   A. Aizer and S. McLanahan, *The Impact of Child Support Enforcement on Fertility, Parental Investment and Child Well Being*, National Bureau of Economic Research, Cambridge, MA, 2005.

at enforcement, but separated mothers are now allowed to keep any child support from non-custodial fathers when they receive in-work benefits – with a proposed extension to out-of-work benefits. Despite assertions that research shows 'little evidence'[9] that this might increase relationship breakdown, those who have investigated the matter report that couples are 'highly responsive to changes in economic circumstances in deciding whether to continue their partnership' and that 'new information with regard to household finances have [sic] a substantial impact on the probability of partnership dissolution'. [10]

Divorce laws and incentives to commit

Whatever the incentives available, or the relative attractions of differing options, a given course of action also depends on what barriers, if any, there are to its realisation, or to its probability of being translated into actuality. The erosion of the significance attached to the married state, and the declining influence of religious, moral and legal obstacles to marital dissolution and illegitimacy, has left individuals freer to respond in the face of the apparent financial advantages and disadvantages of various options. The system put in motion in the late 1960s has meant that there is hardly an agreement that is easier to break without blame attaching to any party, and without the law being able to apportion responsibility and secure compensation for disappointed expectations, than the marriage agreement. This was set

9   Sir David Henshaw's Report to the Secretary of State for Work and Pensions, *Recovering Child Support: Routes to Responsibility*, Presented to Parliament by the Secretary of State for Work and Pensions, Cm. 6894, 2006.

10 I. Walker and Y. Zhu, *Child Support and Partnership Dissolution: Evidence from the UK Dept of Economics*, University of Kent Studies in Economics no. 0408 2004.

to encourage opportunism, lower the costs to departing spouses and remove protection or leverage from those who do not want their marriages to dissolve. Not only need the instigators of divorce incur little or no loss, they might benefit. Norms of loyalty and sharing are weakened and altruistic, family-first, cooperative behaviour is discounted.

Entering marriage with the knowledge, even the expectation, that it may last only a short time means that people may not be inclined to fully commit in a costly and uncertain venture. As it becomes more rational to withhold investment in joint resources and family-specific human capital, so marriages with less invested in them are then more likely to break up.[11] The one who has guarded his or her private interests best will come out best. Newspaper advice to married couples is that 'Maintaining some degree of financial independence is crucial. Married couples should not pool all their assets: keeping separate current and savings accounts will make life much easier if you split up.'[12]

A number of studies find that no-fault divorce laws had a significant impact on divorce rates in the USA and Canada, both long and short term.[13] In 40 years of US census data capturing variations in divorce regulations across states and over time, unilateral divorce appears to have significantly increased the odds of an adult being divorced by about 12 per cent. A child was 15

---

11 S. Grossbard-Shechtman, 'Marriage market models', in M. Tommasi and K. Ier-ulli, *The New Economics of Human Behaviour*, Cambridge University Press, Cambridge, 1996.

12 P. Hawkins, 'The going is getting tougher', *The Times*, 25 June 2003.

13 L. Friedberg, 'Did unilateral divorce rates raise divorce rates? evidence from panel data', *American Economic Review*, 83, 1998, p. 3; J. Wolfers, *Did Unilateral Divorce Laws Raise Divorce Rates? A Reconciliation and New Results*, Working Paper no. 10014, NBER, 2003.

per cent more likely to be living with a divorced mother and 11 per cent more likely to be living with a divorced father than under the old laws, as well as more likely to be living in a lower-income household. The impact of changes in law on behaviour and child outcomes plateaus after eight years.[14] An analysis of trends in eighteen European countries, which controlled for factors that might influence both the law and divorce rates in specific countries, shows that legal reforms account for about 20 per cent of the increase in divorce rates in Europe between 1960 and 2003.[15] For the UK, John Ermisch's work gives a decisive role to divorce reform in explaining the rise in lone parenthood in the 1970s, estimating that the net impact was to increase the percentage of lone-parent families by four percentage points, or about 50 per cent at this time.[16]

As divorce laws ease, and the front-line financial benefits of marriage are removed, a greater proportion of less able people may opt for divorce, people who may be less able to compensate for the absence of a second parent. Moreover, easier divorce not only decreases investment in children following on from parental separation but also changes bargaining power within intact households. Since the least attached spouse has most power under no-fault regulations, they can shift family spending away from child investment towards personal consumption.[17]

Changes in the law have effectively made it impossible for two people to make a substantial commitment, irrevocable without

14 J. Gruber, 'Is making divorce easier bad for children? The long run implications of unilateral divorce', *Journal of Labor Economics*, 22, 2004, pp. 799–833.

15 L. Gonzalez and T. K. Viitanen, *The Effect of Divorce Laws on Divorce Rates in Europe*, Discussion Paper no. 2023, IZA, Bonn, 2006.

16 J. Ermisch, *Lone Parenthood*, Cambridge University Press, Cambridge, 1991.

17 Gruber, 'Is making divorce easier bad for children?'

serious consequences, even if they should wish to do so. As such, these changes in the law have also changed the underlying economics of family life by making it more likely that individuals will change their behaviour in response to changes in incentives within the tax and benefit systems. Messy marital laws as well as the benefits system may also lead people to believe that casual and conditional relationships let them keep their freedom and independence and avoid the restrictions and demands of marriage, economic and otherwise.[18]

It is commitment which changes how men see themselves and how they behave. Only upon marriage does a man publicly assume the responsibilities associated with any consequent parenthood. Cohabiting couples often do not share their income and expect each other to be self-supporting.[19] It is suggested that, where couples feel themselves to be mutually acceptable spouses, they wait to have children within marriage, while a woman may have a child with a man she rejects as a husband.[20] An unmarried pregnant woman is likely to consider herself independent of the father of her child and the father considers himself independent of the woman – who will be cared for by the state, with the decision to have a child outside marriage similar for both women in live-in relationships and those who live apart from the boyfriend.

Increasingly accepted and decreasingly stable, cohabitations involve couples with less and less serious intentions, who live together as a matter of convenience, leading to both lower

---

18 L. L. Bumpass, J. A. Sweet and A. Cherlin, 'The role of cohabitation in declining rates of marriage', *Journal of Marriage and the Family*, 53, 1991, pp. 913–27.

19 D. Del Boca, 'Intrahousehold distribution of resources and labor market participation decisions', in C. Jonung and I. Persson (eds), *Economics of the Family*, Routledge, London, 1997.

20 Ermisch, *An Economic History of Bastardy in England and Wales*.

marriage and higher separation rates.[21] Among women born in the 1950s, about one quarter cohabited in their first live-in relationship. For those born in the 1970s, the figure is 85 per cent. Widespread cohabitation was pioneered first by the more highly educated, who had most financial and occupational incentives to wait before entering a more committed and fertile relationship. It then spread to people who found it convenient to have children in casual associations – given that there is more room to manoeuvre and the prospect of easy exit with changing circumstances and incentives. It is easier for the wage earner not to be officially known at the partner's address for benefit purposes if a couple is cohabiting. This also means, of course, that there is less to hold the unit together or an absence of a supporting structure, and no long-term perspective or commitment to the enterprise of building a life and future together. It is worth noting in passing that legal changes are granting the remaining privileges or rights of marriage (mainly involving inheritance) to cohabitations that lack the responsibilities imposed by marriage.

Cheaper as one

In the last quarter of the twentieth century, couples with children may have found it less easy to improve their economic status and security. In the recent past the cumulative benefits of a marital alliance would have been facilitated by (normally a man's) job security, the higher levels of income earned with age, a more favourable tax position, and lower child-rearing costs.

Overall, consumption resources have since increased less in

---

21 L. Bumpass and H. Lu, 'Trends in cohabitation and implications for children's family contexts in the US', *Population Studies*, 54, 2000, pp. 29–41.

relation to income for couples and large household units than for single people. Families have also had less than average additional purchasing power post-1970, not least owing to heavier tax burdens. Families add less through their own production relative to what they buy in the market, with parents increasing their work efforts to secure net income,[22] even if the lost value of household production might almost equal increased money earnings.[23] This may, at least in part, be as a result of increases in the tax burden leading to a necessity for two people to work and also due to subsidised childcare artificially skewing incentives towards work outside the home.

There have been other factors that have contributed to the relative fall in the economic position of couples compared with single-person households. One-person households stand to gain most from a decline in the relative price of purchased household, labour-saving inputs. Capital goods, such as washing machines, greatly reduce the time needed to run a household. Such labour-saving goods go beyond 'white goods' to include cheap manufactured clothes, ready meals and the like. Since they are unable to source household specialisation and the division of labour, single people have to devote a larger share of their spending to these products. A fall in the price of purchased labour-saving household inputs has a bigger impact on singles vis-à-vis couples, as does a fall in the fixed costs of household maintenance as wages rise. All lower the economic incentives to collaborate. Wage growth and technological progress in the household sector, by making it

22 J. Greenwood and N. Guner, 'Marriage and Divorce since World War II: Analyzing the Role of Technological Progress on the Formation of Households', Unpublished paper, University of Rochester and Pennsylvania State University, 2005.

23 R. Gronau, 'Home production: a forgotten industry', *Review of Economics and Statistics*, 62(3), 1980, pp. 408–16.

easier for young adults to leave the parental home, are credited with, first, encouraging early marriage, followed by casual unions, and then living alone. These specific factors are not a product of government intervention and, of course, such developments have made life easier for larger households too.

In the two and a half decades following 1950, income growth is estimated to have been responsible for at least three-quarters of the increased growth in the propensity of single and widowed people to live alone in this time.[24] Income growth and technological progress may be part of the explanation for fragmentation but, even so, couples have had to work more – not least since their tax position vis-à-vis single and childless people deteriorated considerably from the 1970s.

The effect of growing incomes on fragmentation and the creation of one-person households may have waned somewhat recently, given its self-generated costs, particularly for housing. In 2003, nearly three-fifths of men aged 20–24 lived with parents, compared with a half in 1991.[25] This is being counteracted, however, by the ways in which political processes respond to retard any possible adjustments to behaviour caused by price signals that make fragmentation more expensive. In particular, state and local governments fund emergency and social support services, or substitutes for family or household inputs, which are particularly valuable to people living alone. There are increasingly complex housing schemes with implicit subsidies to make housing more 'affordable' to particular groups, and a more relaxed planning regime for densely packed housing aimed at small units

24   R. T. Michael, V. R. Fuchs and S. R. Scott, 'Changes in the propensity to live alone: 1950–1976', *Demography*, 17, 1980, pp. 39–56.
25   ONS, 'Households and families', *Social Trends*, 34, 2004.

or single people. Changes to the local tax system in the late 1980s and early 1990s were also structured to favour single-household occupation; 'unlike the domestic rates which they replaced, both the Community Charge and the Council Tax were explicitly intended to reduce the cost of a single occupant in a house ...'[26]

Summary

The rhetoric is that the Thatcher government did not like and constantly criticised lone-parent families. The reality is that many fiscal changes at that time and since explicitly favoured two-earner households and single-parent households while making living as a couple with children relatively expensive – particularly when they had one income. Changes to divorce laws reinforced this trend and made it easier for people to respond to financial incentives, created by the government, to split up households or have children without having the means to look after them independent of the state. There have been other background factors such as changes to local government taxation and a bias within the planning regime which have also made it artificially cheaper to live in a single-adult household.

---

26   A. W. Evans and O. M. Hartwich, *Unaffordable Housing: Fables and Myths*, Localis and Policy Exchange, London, 2005.

6   MORE OF THE SAME OR A NEW POLICY APPROACH?

He who is unable to live in society, or who has no need because he is sufficient for himself, must be either a beast or a god.

ARISTOTLE

The mounting costs

Growing family and household fragmentation is a major cause of higher government spending. It is the source of a growing number of clients of the state who have strong incentives to vote for policies that reinforce the incentives for household fragmentation. There are social benefits from stable households, such as less pressure on the environment, on health services, the criminal justice system and social services, yet the state creates incentives that militate against the creation of multi-person households.

The current level of public spending and the taxes to finance it would have been unthinkable early in the last century and, while this began to grow in the 1930s, it rose only slowly until 1960. This spending leads to the atomisation of society since it so often displaces existing institutional or private arrangements and so adds nothing to the level of welfare that people would or could have otherwise received.[1] Instead of the state stepping in where

---

1   V. Tanzi, *A Lower Tax Future?*, Politeia, London, 2004.

the market is unable to provide, the state has increasingly replaced the market.[2] The same surely applies to the family sphere. Increasingly the state is directly assuming the care as much as the support of children; the state considers itself a superior parent as much as a superior provider.

Income support programmes have little positive impact on child development, while a stable family background can have large positive effects on childhood and adult outcomes. In providing incentives to reject marriage, the age-old and universal arrangement most beneficial to children's development, the state is subsidising and so increasing the loss of social capital. More and more reliant upon the state for support, families are also wide open to outside intervention. Government interventions to deal with the collapse of parenting include the New Deal for the Community, Sure Start, Child Care, Anti-Social Behaviour Orders, Acceptable Behaviour Contracts, Parenting Orders and Fixed Penalty Notices, in addition to the deployment of thousands of Community Support Officers on the streets. It is also envisaged that a wide range of authorities should be allowed to apply for parenting orders. As part of a hugely intrusive programme of surveillance, every child will be registered on an electronic database, detailing all contacts with any public service and accessible to all 'experts' working 'for' children.

Since fatherhood outside marriage creates uncertainties, this is also generating an increasing mass of legislation and regulation of provisions for custody, access and financial support. The marriage contract creates the social and economic link between fathers and children. In its absence, public policy is scrabbling to construct involuntary forms of fatherhood to replace the voluntary pattern

2   V. Tanzi and L. Schuknecht, *Public Spending in the Twentieth Century*, Cambridge University Press, Cambridge, 2000.

established by marriage; forms that fail to give children viable and permanent kinship relationships. When parents divorce or never marry, the state becomes involved in requiring or regulating child-rearing obligations that married parents would fulfil voluntarily.

This expansion of professional authorities to replace families as child rearers is, as always, justified on the grounds that the best way to 'help' people is to relieve them of their responsibilities. But it is exceedingly doubtful that any public services can make up for the missing private investment in children, or for the demise of informal social controls. A cynical view might be that the strategy is not really about enriching the lives of children or the 'excluded', but is about extending state power, eroding the sphere of freedom and dissolving intermediate institutions.

The effect of state welfare on income redistribution is small compared with 'family welfare', or the sharing of earnings between family members and other private transfers. The stable family represents the best social welfare system that any community has devised (for lifelong help) and certainly the least expensive. It is wrong to assume that the only income transfers that are made in society are ones that pass via the Treasury, determined by the political process, in the form of social support payments. There is the substantial and far more important voluntary redistribution going on each day within millions of homes between family members. This has access to a knowledge about the needs and ends of different individuals that is denied to government. The internal transactions within families make a major contribution to the reconciliation of justice in exchange with justice in distribution.[3] Reduced multi-person household formation inhibits

---

3   T. Dwyer, *The Taxation of Shared Family Incomes*, Policy Monograph 61, Centre for Independent Study, 2004.

the accumulation of wealth in midlife, something that will have serious implications for ageing societies.

In revisiting Adam Smith's *Theory of the Moral Sentiments*, greater attention has been given recently to the role of informal relations, and the ethos of society (or features of social life – networks, trust, norms, etc.), in the success of economies. People can achieve more together than they do apart. There is a creeping admission that the concentration on education and qualifications, or human capital, like that on physical and financial capital, 'seems unlikely to end poverty and social exclusion, without attention to social, particularly bridging social capital'.[4] Like other forms of capital, this requires investment to build. By its nature this investment must take place at the level of households and the voluntary community, yet the state is displacing this investment as well as increasingly making it more expensive for households to build up such social capital themselves, as welfare dissolves links that once held people together.

More of the same?

What rational defence is there for continuing to favour and encourage through taxation and benefits policies forms of lifestyle that bring with them significant social costs? The situation is all the more extraordinary considering that some of those in the government research orbit have belatedly realised that demographic changes may be a crucial unacknowledged factor in

4   D. Piachaud, *Capital and the Determinants of Poverty and Social Exclusion*, CASE-paper 60, ESRC Sticerd Toyota Centre, London School of Economics, 2002, pp. 19–20; also M. Kleinman, *Include Me Out? The New Politics of Place and Poverty*, CASEpaper 11, Centre for Analysis of Social Exclusion, 1998.

continuing high levels of inequality, and constitute 'substantial challenges to social justice: higher child poverty, increased future care needs, fundamentally altered housing requirements and intensified environmental problems'.[5] But while it is admitted how 'focusing on the benefits of living alone ignores the distributional implications of this trend', there is no recognition that the state may be facilitating movement from relatively cheap and efficient forms of living to comparatively expensive and damaging ones, and so no call for it to desist. While calculations in 2006 were that a two-earner couple earning £10,000 and £25,000 respectively are already £5,473 a year better off if they live apart, under proposals from the Rowntree Foundation for tackling persistent child poverty through bigger tax credits they could be £7,500 a year better off.[6] Since this will continue to undermine two-parent families, it will help to perpetuate the cycle of poverty. The Institute for Public Policy Research (IPPR) is not interested in reducing child poverty if this means encouraging the formation and maintenance of stable families. Rather it describes the way in which '… the lack of a progressive response to demography has severely constrained the Government's ability to articulate a convincing response to anachronistic demands for greater support for traditional families rather than lone parents, when it is single mothers who are most in need of support'.[7]

Their answer is a 'progressive response', by a 'progressive government', with a 'progressive approach' that will 'allow progressives to take the international lead' and define 'new

---

5   M. Dixon and J. Margo, *Population and Politics*, Institute for Public Policy Research, 2006, p. 4.

6   Institute for Fiscal Studies press release, March 2006, and 'What will it take to end child poverty?', Joseph Rowntree Foundation, 2006.

7   Dixon and Margo, *Population and Politics*, pp. 82 and 52.

political territory on their own progressive terms', while 'leading public opinion in a progressive direction'. The first 'progressive policy response' demanded is the appointment of a Minister for Demography, Migration and Citizenship. As we must mitigate the 'negative effects' of demographic trends, one way is to '... reinforce support for traditional progressive goals, such as universal childcare and investment in the early years ...' In turn, single living is meant to be addressed in an 'enabling way'. More services and personal assistants 'tailored more accurately to their needs' are required for single people less able to call on friends or family for informal support and more therapeutic services to help people as they move in and out of relationships. As one-person households have low employment rates, more apparently needs to be known about the 'labour market barriers' faced by people living alone – when the evidence is already clear and it points to the lack of motivation, pressure and responsibilities. While there is recognition that areas with high levels of single-person households tend to be high crime areas, we are urged to move away from any focus on reducing the volume of crime towards one of reducing the effects of *the experience of crime* on people. The lack of spousal care in old age is lamented, alongside the tendencies of single men to smoke, drink too much, take less care of themselves than married men, die alone and have no one to arrange a funeral. So, ambitiously, the government is also called upon '... to design, renovate and reinvigorate communities in a way that facilitates levels of community participation by people living alone' and conjure up social and emotional support networks.

What would not be acceptable to these 'progressive' authors is encouraging family life by, for example, child allowances for rearing children at home. Tax allowances (for adult dependants) that might go to the main wage earner would be equally unpalatable. These authors express horror at the French policy of giving women with small children large family allowances to spend on any form of care they want, since more mothers have left work for a time to care for their families at home. Joint pensions are condemned for making 'anachronistic assumptions about family structure'. Instead, childcare provision and parental leave (for men) will somehow '… help people meet their demographic aspirations [sic] in a way that would reduce future poverty, inequality and care needs', when it is precisely two-income couples, along with more lone parents, who are pulling the income distribution apart.[8] While much is made of how support for married couples would be a terrible imposition on people, or 'nannying', which somehow deprives them of choice, the only choice deemed worthy of support is one where women work full time with their children in day care, since this helps to move us towards the goal of gender parity in pay and position. While it is accepted that greater involvement by the father is beneficial for children's development, this is to be secured not via marriage but by parental leave, where men contribute not by earning but by doing more domestic chores.

Far from the French model 'not being acceptable in the UK', study after study shows that only a small proportion of women want continual full-time work while they are rearing children.

Sadly, most intellectual and political opinion insists that solutions lie in more of the kind of intervention that is already busily promoting social dislocation and disintegration. Occasionally, there is a glint of recognition that the 'behaviour of household

---

8   Ibid., pp. 67, 102, 112 and 182.

members in protecting individuals' from economic misfortune is important, so perhaps 'policies ... will need to address such factors ...'[9] But, since marriage is too indelicate or explosive a subject to raise in academic company, this usually means tiptoeing around the blindingly obvious:

> Living in larger households helps individuals at staying out of poverty, with a coefficient that is larger in absolute value than for the exit rate. This seems to confirm the idea that income accruing to members other than the household head is [an] important means to keep the household above the poverty line. This finding has also been highlighted by the cross tabulation analysis of Jenkins (1999) and OECD (1998) and suggests that policies that encourage two-earner households (subsidised child care, tax breaks for second earner, etc.) can have an important role ...[10]

Something better?

The benefits to society of family commitments within households, including marriage, are so huge that these institutions should be nurtured rather than eradicated. There is no need to denigrate other 'lifestyles': the tax and benefits system should just stop discouraging family commitment and treating it as superfluous. It has come to a truly shocking state of affairs when perfectly compatible married people are living separately, or pretending to do so,

---

9   S. Burgess, K. Gardiner and C. Propper, *Why Rising Tides Don't Lift All Boats? An examination of the relationship between poverty and unemployment in Britain*, CASE-paper 46, ESRC Sticerd Toyota Centre, London School of Economics, 2001, p. 33.

10   F. Devicienti, *Poverty Persistence in Britain: A Multivariate Analysis Using the BHPS, 1991–1997*, Institute for Social and Economic Research, 2000, p. 15.

so that they do not lose benefits.[11] Most people view marriage as a desirable goal. A youth worker on inner-city estates observes how: 'If you talk to young people, they all support marriage. There are very few who say they wouldn't get married, especially among women.'[12]

Individuals have to be helped to honour any long-term contract. There needs to be support and encouragement for commitment, and costs should be borne by those who unilaterally and unreasonably dissolve their unions.[13] Since no-fault divorce has eroded incentives for long-term commitment, this should be restricted to circumstances where both spouses agree to the basis and terms of separation. Consensual divorce would enable each spouse to bargain from a position of equality, protect people from expropriation of their investments in the marriage, and deter opportunism.[14] Unilateral divorce would no longer apply. Instead, grounds of fault could enable 'wronged' spouses to claim compensation by way of a differential property settlement or maintenance. It cannot be stressed too strongly that this is not the institutionalisation of a certain form of traditionalism. It is simply ensuring that the agreements that people have made are enforced. This is a *liberal* position in the true sense of the word. It would involve the proper enforcement of contracts that are freely entered (with consensual termination as with other forms of

11   G. Dench, K. Gavron and M. Young, *The New East End*, Profile Books, London, 2006.

12   S. Bailey, *No Man's Land: How Britain's inner city young are being failed*, Centre for Young Policy Studies, 2005, p. 21.

13   E. S. Scott, 'Marital commitment and regulation of divorce', in R. Rowthorn and A. Dines (eds), *The Law and Economics of Marriage and Divorce*, Cambridge University Press, Cambridge, 2002, and B. Maley, *Divorce Law and the Future of Marriage*, CIS Policy Monograph 58, 2003.

14   Rowthorn and Dines, *The Law and Economics of Marriage and Divorce*.

contract), and proper compensation for parties hurt by those who walk away from such contracts.

The other side of the coin to stronger exit barriers is sharp legal boundaries, with well-defined restrictions, obligations and privileges that delineate a relationship of binding legal commitment. The legal trend is to impose rights and restrictions upon cohabiting couples, *in the manner of compulsory marriage for people who do not want to be married*. This overlooks the way in which people are cohabiting, partly because the law has been made dysfunctional through the abolition of any legal commitment mechanism. Marriage can hardly exist unless it confers privileges and imposes obligations different from those on people who elect to cohabit or associate in some other way. People who do not wish to have the responsibilities of marriage should not have its rights and responsibilities thrust upon them – no more than they should expect other taxpayers to meet the financial costs of their decisions related to children, residence and so forth.

Tough enforcement of child support would diminish the financial scope for separated parents to have more children without providing adequately for those that already exist. Theory and evidence suggest that both the attractions of non-marital fatherhood, and the proportion of children born out of wedlock would decrease if child support were strictly enforced.[15] The responsibility for existing children would then take precedence over the possibility of having further children. The non-resident parent(s) should be the first port of call for child maintenance, not the state or the public purse. All maintenance payments to lone parents should be treated as income for benefit and tax purposes, on a

---

15 R. J. Willis, 'A theory of out of wedlock childbearing', *Journal of Political Economy*, 107, 1999, pp. S33–S64.

par with the income of parents who live together, to ensure equal treatment.

Marriage and other family commitments lead to lower burdens on the state because family members transfer income between themselves. The 'financial change of direction away from the support of marriage has created a wasted opportunity to support a section of the public whose value to society has been seriously undervalued', so this should be rectified – not least by removing the unjust penalties on intact families from the tax and benefit systems. Virtually the only remaining advantage of marriage relates to taxes on capital gains and at death, which have little reference to care for dependants or mutual support and little relevance to most families on average incomes or below.

Economic support for marriage has to be front-loaded. While some may wish to affirmatively promote marriage through the structure of public benefit programmes, there is probably more agreement and a stronger case that programmes should not penalise or discourage marriage. Claims that this would constitute interference in private decisions involving relationships are invalidated not least by the way in which the tax and benefit systems gives bonuses to mothers who stay single, and impose substantial penalties on lower- and now middle-income couples who live in the same household. To argue that the government has an obligation to support lone parents and spend vast sums mitigating the damage that results from the erosion of marriage – but should do nothing to support marriage itself – is like arguing that government should pay to sustain lung cancer victims but not to discourage smoking, or that insurance companies should ask higher premiums from those who do not drive dangerously. To argue that assets are important for long-term welfare and life chances and then to reduce the amount by half for a married couple compared with two singles before they lose state benefits is to maliciously sabotage mutual endeavour for mutual advantage.

Means-tested benefits: money going round in circles

The tax and/or benefits position of two-parent families, including those outside the welfare system, must be improved to remove the subsidy to alternative forms of living. If two-parent families become more economically secure they will be more viable and, as their status improves, so the desirability of marrying, having children as a couple and remaining together will increase.[16] As it happens, much of this can be achieved through less government interference and manipulation.

The analysis points to a return to universal and equitable family income protection. Income-based or means-tested transfers are not effective in enhancing living standards, since they disincentivise self-improvement and mutual support and, in so doing, contribute to and entrench poverty. The use and level of needs-based safety nets ought to be minimal. In what has become a staggeringly complex system, money is taken away from people before they have secured their basic subsistence; then handed out in benefits, with considerable leakage along the way from bureaucracy, errors and fraud (the baffling obscurity of the Australian tax credit system, with its overpayments and unintelligibility, was already apparent when Gordon Brown insisted on forging ahead with a similar system in the UK). In all this churning many people are made welfare-dependent when their earnings, before tax,

16   D. T. Ellwood, *Poor Support: Poverty and the American Family*, Basic Books, New York, 1988.

often go all or a long way to meet family requirements. If a family is deemed so wealthy that it can afford to pay tax then it should not be receiving welfare assistance, and a family poor enough to be receiving welfare assistance ought not to be paying tax.

Where possible, people should not be taxpayers and benefit recipients at the same time. Instead of extending the reach and increasing the clientele for benefits or tax credits, households should keep more of their original income. The basic tax allowance must be raised above the welfare floor as the first step towards reducing churning and restoring incentives.

Social housing and benefits to pay rent have played a massive part in the causation of a (now) inter-generational process of social disintegration and decay; reversing the process seen in the immediate post-war decades, when underclass membership was declining. This calls for an urgent review of how social housing is allocated and paid for. It is grossly unfair that housing is automatically granted to those with children who are below a certain income level, while others must postpone their childbearing until they can acquire a home by their own efforts. It has meant that '... the whole moral order has become inverted by the emphasis placed by the state on individual need. For if what one gets out of the state is determined by need, rather than by what one has put into it, then dignity has been taken out of citizenship. Dependency is encouraged, the principle of reciprocity has gone ...'[17] Housing for poorer people should again become a base upon which to build. It should be available only on a more restricted basis and on more worthy and responsible criteria than those of estrangement and helplessness. A housing benefit that is in addition to or separate from a

17   Dench et al., *The New East End*, p. 209.

basic welfare safety net should be abolished. If this necessitates a return to 'subsidising bricks, not people', then so be it.

Consistency in the tax and benefits systems

Although the welfare system assesses income at a family level, the tax system treats people as single income units. There are few developed countries where no tax allowance is made for family responsibilities. No matter how many people might share in an income, the provider carries the cost in the UK with only one tax allowance, even given that spouses have a legal right to be supported by each other, and their benefits are withdrawn or reduced when they do so. Couples where two earners choose to work outside the home receive two tax allowances. While the tax system does not recognise that one income can be supporting more than one person, the benefits system explicitly does so. Thus the single-earner couple does not receive benefits if their aggregate income is above means-tested benefit levels. On the other hand the non-earner in the same couple, on the same aggregate income, would receive benefits if the couple split up. The demoralising effect is that taxpayers shed dependants upon the social security system or collude with dependants to pick up from the welfare system what the tax system takes away from them. This collusion frequently involves explicit fraud.

There are two ways of addressing this problem. All individuals, regardless of whether they are married to an earner, could receive a guaranteed minimum income from the state – in other words, the benefits system, like the tax system, could cease to recognise the concept of intra-household support. Increasingly, this is happening with state pension provision, where credits are being given to non-earners with caring responsibilities. The objection to this is both cost and the fact that it would make non-earners in single-earner couples more dependent on the state for their income, with reciprocity and interdependence devalued and undermined. We must remember that tax and benefits systems send messages as well as move money.

Alternatively, adjustments could be made to the tax system so that, like the benefits system, it recognises the concept of a household. Families should be allowed to retain resources on a par with those available to individuals without dependants, probably through transferring tax-free entitlements. Alternatively, a household could be allowed to split the combined income into a number of 'slices', with each slice being allocated to a dependant and taxed as the income of that dependant.[18] The aim should be to offer a much lower deduction rate within reach of the working family which is close to average male full-time earnings.[19] While means-tested payments give people incentives not to work, declare income or marry, tax allowances reduce the perverse incentives to inactivity, family breakdown and male abdication created by targeted benefits. If means testing has to survive for working families, then it is necessary to lengthen the phase-out range or taper for married couples, by giving them an income disregard.

These suggestions may meet with the complaint that single people will, comparatively if not absolutely, pay more or receive less – to which it is possible to retort that 'they are less likely to be engaged in the reciprocal support activities of the moral economy

18   See M. Nicholson, *Keep It Simple: Proposals to Reduce the Complexity of the UK Tax System*, Bow Group, 2006.

19   M. Saatchi and P. Warburton, *Poor People! Stop Paying Tax!*, Centre for Policy Studies, London, 2001.

which limit the collective liabilities of the welfare state'.[20] Genuine neutrality in taxation is not possible unless this recognises private income arrangements within families, just as it recognises income sharing in business partnerships.

If it is felt that 'rich' families are not being taxed sufficiently, the remedy is to adjust the gradation of the tax scales, so that the rich, including the rich without families, are equally affected. In this murky area of argument, the designation 'rich' moves too easily from the couple in the stately home to any couple above the income support line to any couple at all, so that only stand-alone mothers are left as worthy objects of assistance.

Political masters out of touch

Antipathy to one-income couples is at the heart of much anti-marriage and anti-two-parent bias, with earner fathers represented as antisocial and bad for family life. The reality is that working fathers help to lift families out of poverty and improve children's life chances, just as fathers living within families make better citizens and workers than those outside. This involves a familiar form of interpersonal care and support, where the preferences of academics and politicians are quite at variance with those of the bulk of the population. From an unlikely source, a review of nineteen projects in the Joseph Rowntree Foundation programme Work and Family Life, from 1997 to 2003, concluded that: 'policy and benefit regimes have been largely ignoring ... mainstream middle ground family life in Britain'. Survey after survey suggested that 'many mothers' preferences run counter to the

20   G. Dench and B. Brown, *Towards a New Partnership between Family and State (The Grandmother Project)*, Institute of Community Studies, 2004, p. 49.

direction Government policy is trying to encourage ...' and that the emphasis on maternal employment 'reinforces the low value placed on unpaid work and care' and suggests that 'paid child care is better than parental care'.[21]

A further anomaly in the current tax system is that it treats family income earned by a second earner more favourably than, for example, overtime or promotion of the primary earner, assuming that the primary earner is in a higher tax bracket than the secondary earner. This and related factors may well contribute to a growth in maternal labour force participation beyond the point of choice. Present policies bypass the wishes of the majority and make it harder for them to run their lives as they wish. Improvements in the employment status and economic viability of men (as much as or more than those of mothers) are necessary to reduce levels of lone parenthood (as well as crime).[22] A study of welfare reform in Minnesota demonstrated how improving families' financial security improved their chances of becoming and staying married.[23] Marriage- and earnings-enhancing policies can together set off a virtuous circle,[24] whose attainment requires an end to the denigration of fathers who work to support their children.

21 S. Dex, 'Families and work in the twenty first century', *Foundations*, Joseph Rowntree Foundation, York, 2003.

22 H. F. Myers, 'Commentary', in M. B. Tucker and C. Mitchell-Kerman, *The Decline in Marriage among African Americans*, Russell Sage Foundation, New York, 1995.

23 V. Knox, C. Miller and L. Gennetian, 'Reforming welfare and rewarding work: a summary of the final report on the Minnesota family investment program', Manpower Demonstration Research Corporation, New York, 2000.

24 A. Ahituv and R. I. Lerman, *How Do Marital Status, Wage Rates, and Work Commitment Interact?*, Discussion Paper 1688, Institute for the Study of Labor, Bonn, 2005.

Wider horizons

Even before the state cast its preference for lone parenthood, public policy ignored the extent to which nuclear families were founded in wider kinship ties. Should we not give greater recognition to descent, and to the continuing role of family elders as influential supporters of younger adults? It might generally be cost effective to reinforce the reciprocity between generations as a prolific source of support and a model for good citizenship and public civility.[25]

Since co-residence is an efficient use of resources, policy incentives to encourage older people to live with or very near younger relatives might improve the elders' income position as well.[26] It is an incredible state of affairs when a householder can be charged an extra 33 per cent council tax when they are supporting a dependent adult, whether it is a non-earning wife or a grown-up child, even for the shortest time, yet they will be exempted from this if the extra adult(s) either leaves or goes on benefit. There are grounds here for discriminating in favour of multi-person households, and ending subsidies for under-occupation or, at the very least, of not discouraging multi-occupation. This and other moves could encourage people to get support through families and reduce dependence on direct benefits, in particular those that set claimants up as independent households at public expense. More needs to be done to ascertain how resource sharing could be encouraged, whether between related individuals or not. Voluntary action within and between families and households should be the first source of welfare.

---

25 A. Zaidi, J. R. Frick and F. Buchel, *Income Mobility in Old Age in Britain and Germany*, CASEpaper 89, ESRC Sticerd Toyota Centre, London School of Economics, 2004.

26 Dench and Brown, *Towards a New Partnership*.

ABOUT THE IEA

The Institute is a research and educational charity (No. CC 235 351), limited by guarantee. Its mission is to improve understanding of the fundamental institutions of a free society by analysing and expounding the role of markets in solving economic and social problems.

The IEA achieves its mission by:

- a high-quality publishing programme
- conferences, seminars, lectures and other events
- outreach to school and college students
- brokering media introductions and appearances

The IEA, which was established in 1955 by the late Sir Antony Fisher, is an educational charity, not a political organisation. It is independent of any political party or group and does not carry on activities intended to affect support for any political party or candidate in any election or referendum, or at any other time. It is financed by sales of publications, conference fees and voluntary donations.

In addition to its main series of publications the IEA also publishes a quarterly journal, *Economic Affairs*.

The IEA is aided in its work by a distinguished international Academic Advisory Council and an eminent panel of Honorary Fellows. Together with other academics, they review prospective IEA publications, their comments being passed on anonymously to authors. All IEA papers are therefore subject to the same rigorous independent refereeing process as used by leading academic journals.

IEA publications enjoy widespread classroom use and course adoptions in schools and universities. They are also sold throughout the world and often translated/reprinted.

Since 1974 the IEA has helped to create a world-wide network of 100 similar institutions in over 70 countries. They are all independent but share the IEA's mission.

Views expressed in the IEA's publications are those of the authors, not those of the Institute (which has no corporate view), its Managing Trustees, Academic Advisory Council members or senior staff.

Members of the Institute's Academic Advisory Council, Honorary Fellows, Trustees and Staff are listed on the following page.

The Institute gratefully acknowledges financial support for its publications programme and other work from a generous benefaction by the late Alec and Beryl Warren.

The Institute of Economic Affairs
2 Lord North Street, Westminster, London SW1P 3LB
Tel: 020 7799 8900
Fax: 020 7799 2137
Email: iea@iea.org.uk
Internet: iea.org.uk

155

Other papers recently published by the IEA include:

WHO, What and Why?
Transnational Government, Legitimacy and the World Health Organization
Roger Scruton
Occasional Paper 113; ISBN 0 255 36487 3; £8.00

The World Turned Rightside Up
A New Trading Agenda for the Age of Globalisation
John C. Hulsman
Occasional Paper 114; ISBN 0 255 36495 4; £8.00

The Representation of Business in English Literature
Introduced and edited by Arthur Pollard
Readings 53; ISBN 0 255 36491 1; £12.00

Anti-Liberalism 2000
The Rise of New Millennium Collectivism
David Henderson
Occasional Paper 115; ISBN 0 255 36497 0; £7.50

Capitalism, Morality and Markets
Brian Griffiths, Robert A. Sirico, Norman Barry & Frank Field
Readings 54; ISBN 0 255 36496 2; £7.50

A Conversation with Harris and Seldon
Ralph Harris & Arthur Seldon
Occasional Paper 116; ISBN 0 255 36498 9; £7.50

Malaria and the DDT Story
Richard Tren & Roger Bate
Occasional Paper 117; ISBN 0 255 36499 7; £10.00

A Plea to Economists Who Favour Liberty: Assist the Everyman
Daniel B. Klein
Occasional Paper 118; ISBN 0 255 36501 2; £10.00

The Changing Fortunes of Economic Liberalism
Yesterday, Today and Tomorrow
David Henderson
Occasional Paper 105 (new edition); ISBN 0 255 36520 9; £12.50

The Global Education Industry
Lessons from Private Education in Developing Countries
James Tooley
Hobart Paper 141 (new edition); ISBN 0 255 36503 9; £12.50

Saving Our Streams
The Role of the Anglers' Conservation Association in
Protecting English and Welsh Rivers
Roger Bate
Research Monograph 53; ISBN 0 255 36494 6; £10.00

Better Off Out?
The Benefits or Costs of EU Membership
Brian Hindley & Martin Howe
Occasional Paper 99 (new edition); ISBN 0 255 36502 0; £10.00

Buckingham at 25
Freeing the Universities from State Control
Edited by James Tooley
Readings 55; ISBN 0 255 36512 8; £15.00

Lectures on Regulatory and Competition Policy
Irwin M. Stelzer
Occasional Paper 120; ISBN 0 255 36511 X; £12.50

Misguided Virtue
False Notions of Corporate Social Responsibility
David Henderson
Hobart Paper 142; ISBN 0 255 36510 1; £12.50

HIV and Aids in Schools
The Political Economy of Pressure Groups and Miseducation
Barrie Craven, Pauline Dixon, Gordon Stewart & James Tooley
Occasional Paper 121; ISBN 0 255 36522 5; £10.00

The Road to Serfdom
The Reader's Digest *condensed version*
Friedrich A. Hayek
Occasional Paper 122; ISBN 0 255 36530 6; £7.50

Bastiat's *The Law*
Introduction by Norman Barry
Occasional Paper 123; ISBN 0 255 36509 8; £7.50

A Globalist Manifesto for Public Policy
Charles Calomiris
Occasional Paper 124; ISBN 0 255 36525 X; £7.50

Euthanasia for Death Duties
Putting Inheritance Tax Out of Its Misery
Barry Bracewell-Milnes
Research Monograph 54; ISBN 0 255 36513 6; £10.00

Liberating the Land
The Case for Private Land-use Planning
Mark Pennington
Hobart Paper 143; ISBN 0 255 36508 X; £10.00

IEA Yearbook of Government Performance 2002/2003
Edited by Peter Warburton
Yearbook 1; ISBN 0 255 36532 2; £15.00

Britain's Relative Economic Performance, 1870–1999
Nicholas Crafts
Research Monograph 55; ISBN 0 255 36524 1; £10.00

Should We Have Faith in Central Banks?
Otmar Issing
Occasional Paper 125; ISBN 0 255 36528 4; £7.50

The Dilemma of Democracy
Arthur Seldon
Hobart Paper 136 (reissue); ISBN 0 255 36536 5; £10.00

Capital Controls: a 'Cure' Worse Than the Problem?
Forrest Capie
Research Monograph 56; ISBN 0 255 36506 3; £10.00

The Poverty of 'Development Economics'
Deepak Lal
Hobart Paper 144 (reissue); ISBN 0 255 36519 5; £15.00

Should Britain Join the Euro?
The Chancellor's Five Tests Examined
Patrick Minford
Occasional Paper 126; ISBN 0 255 36527 6; £7.50

Post-Communist Transition: Some Lessons
Leszek Balcerowicz
Occasional Paper 127; ISBN 0 255 36533 0; £7.50

A Tribute to Peter Bauer
John Blundell et al.
Occasional Paper 128; ISBN 0 255 36531 4; £10.00

Employment Tribunals
Their Growth and the Case for Radical Reform
J. R. Shackleton
Hobart Paper 145; ISBN 0 255 36515 2; £10.00

Fifty Economic Fallacies Exposed
Geoffrey E. Wood
Occasional Paper 129; ISBN 0 255 36518 7; £12.50

A Market in Airport Slots

Keith Boyfield (editor), David Starkie, Tom Bass & Barry Humphreys
Readings 56; ISBN 0 255 36505 5; £10.00

Money, Inflation and the Constitutional Position of the Central Bank

Milton Friedman & Charles A. E. Goodhart
Readings 57; ISBN 0 255 36538 1; £10.00

railway.com

Parallels between the Early British Railways and the ICT Revolution
Robert C. B. Miller
Research Monograph 57; ISBN 0 255 36534 9; £12.50

The Regulation of Financial Markets

Edited by Philip Booth & David Currie
Readings 58; ISBN 0 255 36551 9; £12.50

Climate Alarmism Reconsidered

Robert L. Bradley Jr
Hobart Paper 146; ISBN 0 255 36541 1; £12.50

Government Failure: E. G. West on Education

Edited by James Tooley & James Stanfield
Occasional Paper 130; ISBN 0 255 36552 7; £12.50

Waging the War of Ideas

John Blundell
Second edition
Occasional Paper 131; ISBN 0 255 36547 0; £12.50

Corporate Governance: Accountability in the Marketplace

Elaine Sternberg
Second edition
Hobart Paper 147; ISBN 0 255 36542 x; £12.50

The Land Use Planning System
Evaluating Options for Reform
John Corkindale
Hobart Paper 148; ISBN 0 255 36550 0; £10.00

Economy and Virtue
Essays on the Theme of Markets and Morality
Edited by Dennis O'Keeffe
Readings 59; ISBN 0 255 36504 7; £12.50

Free Markets Under Siege
Cartels, Politics and Social Welfare
Richard A. Epstein
Occasional Paper 132; ISBN 0 255 36553 5; £10.00

Unshackling Accountants
D. R. Myddelton
Hobart Paper 149; ISBN 0 255 36559 4; £12.50

The Euro as Politics
Pedro Schwartz
Research Monograph 58; ISBN 0 255 36535 7; £12.50

Pricing Our Roads
Vision and Reality
Stephen Glaister & Daniel J. Graham
Research Monograph 59; ISBN 0 255 36562 4; £10.00

The Role of Business in the Modern World
Progress, Pressures, and Prospects for the Market Economy
David Henderson
Hobart Paper 150; ISBN 0 255 36548 9; £12.50

Public Service Broadcasting Without the BBC?
Alan Peacock
Occasional Paper 133; ISBN 0 255 36565 9; £10.00

The ECB and the Euro: the First Five Years
Otmar Issing
Occasional Paper 134; ISBN 0 255 36555 1; £10.00

Towards a Liberal Utopia?
Edited by Philip Booth
Hobart Paperback 32; ISBN 0 255 36563 2; £15.00

The Way Out of the Pensions Quagmire
Philip Booth & Deborah Cooper
Research Monograph 60; ISBN 0 255 36517 9; £12.50

Black Wednesday
A Re-examination of Britain's Experience in the Exchange Rate Mechanism
Alan Budd
Occasional Paper 135; ISBN 0 255 36566 7; £7.50

Crime: Economic Incentives and Social Networks
Paul Ormerod
Hobart Paper 151; ISBN 0 255 36554 3; £10.00

The Road to Serfdom *with* **The Intellectuals and Socialism**
Friedrich A. Hayek
Occasional Paper 136; ISBN 0 255 36576 4; £10.00

Money and Asset Prices in Boom and Bust
Tim Congdon
Hobart Paper 152; ISBN 0 255 36570 5; £10.00

The Dangers of Bus Re-regulation
and Other Perspectives on Markets in Transport
John Hibbs et al.
Occasional Paper 137; ISBN 0 255 36572 1; £10.00

The New Rural Economy
Change, Dynamism and Government Policy
Berkeley Hill et al.
Occasional Paper 138; ISBN 0 255 36546 2; £15.00

The Benefits of Tax Competition
Richard Teather
Hobart Paper 153; ISBN 0 255 36569 1; £12.50

Wheels of Fortune
Self-funding Infrastructure and the Free Market Case for a Land Tax
Fred Harrison
Hobart Paper 154; ISBN 0 255 36589 6; £12.50

Were 364 Economists All Wrong?
Edited by Philip Booth
Readings 60
ISBN-10: 0 255 36588 8; ISBN-13: 978 0 255 36588 8; £10.00

Europe After the 'No' Votes
Mapping a New Economic Path
Patrick A. Messerlin
Occasional Paper 139
ISBN-10: 0 255 36580 2; ISBN-13: 978 0 255 36580 2; £10.00

The Railways, the Market and the Government
John Hibbs et al.
Readings 61
ISBN-10: 0 255 36567 5; ISBN-13: 978 0 255 36567 3; £12.50

Corruption: The World's Big C
Cases, Causes, Consequences, Cures
Ian Senior
Research Monograph 61
ISBN-10: 0 255 36571 3; ISBN-13: 978 0 255 36571 0; £12.50

Sir Humphrey's Legacy
Facing Up to the Cost of Public Sector Pensions
Neil Record
Hobart Paper 156
ISBN-10: 0 255 36578 0; ISBN-13: 978 0 255 36578 9; £10.00

The Economics of Law
Cento Veljanovski
Second edition
Hobart Paper 157
ISBN-10: 0 255 36561 6; ISBN-13: 978 0 255 36561 1; £12.50

Living with Leviathan
Public Spending, Taxes and Economic Performance
David B. Smith
Hobart Paper 158
ISBN-10: 0 255 36579 9; ISBN-13: 978 0 255 36579 6; £12.50

The Vote Motive
Gordon Tullock
New edition
Hobart Paperback 33
ISBN-10: 0 255 36577 2; ISBN-13: 978 0 255 36577 2; £10.00

Waging the War of Ideas
John Blundell
Third edition
Occasional Paper 131
ISBN-10: 0 255 36606 X; ISBN-13: 978 0 255 36606 9; £12.50

To order copies of currently available IEA papers, or to enquire about availability, please contact:

Gazelle
IEA orders
FREEPOST RLYS-EAHU-YSCZ
White Cross Mills
Hightown
Lancaster LA1 4XS

Tel: 01524 68765
Fax: 01524 63232
Email: sales@gazellebooks.co.uk

The IEA also offers a subscription service to its publications. For a single annual payment, currently £40.00 in the UK, you will receive every monograph the IEA publishes during the course of a year and discounts on our extensive back catalogue. For more information, please contact:

Adam Myers
Subscriptions
The Institute of Economic Affairs
2 Lord North Street
London SW1P 3LB

Tel: 020 7799 8920
Fax: 020 7799 2137
Website: www.iea.org.uk